248

WHERE HAVE YOU
GONE, GOD?

Centre for
Faith and Spirituality
Loughborough University

By the same author:

Beyond Healing
God's Gloves

WHERE HAVE YOU GONE, GOD?

Jennifer Rees Larcombe

HODDER AND STOUGHTON
LONDON SYDNEY AUCKLAND TORONTO

All scripture quotations are from the
Good News Bible, unless otherwise stated.
The following abbreviations are used:

Amplified Bible – AMP
Authorised Version – AV
Living Bible – LB
New International Version – NIV

British Library Cataloguing in Publication Data

Rees Larcombe, Jennifer
    Where have you gone, God?
    1. Christian life – Personal observations
    I. Title
    248.4

    ISBN 0-340-50274-6

'Jesus was led by the Spirit into the desert. (Luke 4:1) The best of God's saints have their deserts. The dearest of His children have to walk through a weary wilderness. There is no believer who can always sing for joy. But the Spirit Who led Him was with Him and He is always with us.'
Charles Haddon Spurgeon

CONTENTS

PREFACE:

PLEASE DON'T THROW THIS
BOOK IN THE DUSTBIN

When you feel dried up and dead inside – dazed by suffering, or just plain angry with God – the last thing you want is a theological tome on how to cope! Somebody gave me one when I was first disabled, and in disgust, I threw it straight in the dustbin. All I wanted was to know someone else knew how I was feeling – and really *minded*.

So often Christians are denied this comfort. When we try to tell our friends that our faith has shrivelled like an autumn leaf, they either refuse to take us seriously, or treat us to a barrage of clichés that set our teeth on edge. Worse still, they may write us off as unspiritual, sin-ridden failures!

It is unfashionable to have problems in this success-orientated age, yet loving and obeying God in this world has always had its painful moments and understanding Him is at times quite impossible. Because many Christians have recently discovered a new joy and reality in the life of the church, it makes the dull patches feel even worse. Now we have realised God still heals and delivers miraculously, it is all the harder to understand why He sometimes appears to look the other way when we need Him most.

I never expected to have another 'spiritual desert' after I was filled with the Holy Spirit, so I was devastated. I thought I was the only person who felt mistreated and abandoned by God but over the last two years I have discovered dozens of other Christians who have gone through similar 'dark nights of the soul'. Far from destroying our faith, we have come out on the far side, knowing and loving God in a deeper and more durable way.

Only people who have lived through this experience can possibly understand others who are still trapped inside it. So I have written this book in the hope that it will be the personal contact that so many of us need. It is simply a patchwork of the things I have gleaned from people who know from bitter experience what they are talking about.

We do not offer pat answers to spiritual dryness or despair because there are none. But reading about the mistakes we have made could possibly save you from falling into the same holes! Our practical, coping strategies and escape routes might also prove helpful, but most of all we want to share with you the granite fact that spiritual deserts do not last for ever. Often they are the prelude to something new and exciting. I hope and pray that this book will help you to find the courage to keep going until you discover it.

Don't try and read this book right through if you happen to be in this difficult situation. I have broken it up into short sections, which are clearly labelled so that you can find your way quickly to the topics that interest you most, treating them like mouthfuls of desert manna!

> *How much longer will you forget me, Lord? For ever? How much longer will you hide yourself from me? How long will sorrow fill my heart day and night? I rely on your constant love: I will be glad because you will rescue me. Psalm 13*

ACKNOWLEDGMENTS

More than a thousand people have helped me to write *Where have you gone, God?* If I listed them all there would be no room for a book! Yet, without their time, honesty and prayer, it could never have been written. Some of them have generously allowed me to share with you their deepest experiences, and in a few cases I have changed their names in order to respect their privacy.

Throughout the book's slow evolution Dr Marion Ashton, the Reverend George Swannell, the Reverend Peter Larcombe, Evelyn Shakeshaft, Tony Larcombe, Ann Frost, Shirley Vickers and Lyn Akehurst have offered me invaluable advice and encouragement. My cousin Karen Sinclair spent two weeks with me going through every word with a fine tooth comb.

It is no fun living with someone who is writing a book, but my longsuffering family have generously allowed me the peace and understanding I needed so badly, while my eldest son Justyn even gave up his summer holiday to take his two small brothers off my hands.

Most of all I want to thank my prayer partner Eileen Dymond. For nearly two years she has prayed daily, not only for me as I write, but for every one of you who reads this book.

Still persuade us to rejoice in the deserts of the heart. W. H. Auden

1

WHAT IS A SPIRITUAL DESERT?

'Don't hide yourself from me . . . You have been
my help; don't leave me, . . . , O God, my Saviour.'
Psalm 27:9

Dear Jen,

Help! Something's gone wrong and I'm not quite sure
what! I'm not ill or depressed, I just feel God has
withdrawn Himself from me. I go to church and house
group, but I'm a fly on the wall, not *part* of what's going
on. Prayer is like talking on the phone to someone
who's hung up. I'm just as busy as ever with church
activities, but leading the youth group is such a grind
these days now my enthusiasm's all gone.

It wouldn't be so bad if I could blame all this on to
something, but the circumstances of our lives are as
happy as ever. Outwardly I'm functioning normally,
but inside I know I've lost my joy. So I dread church
now because everyone there looks so maddeningly
happy, all the clapping and singing make me feel I'm
being rubbed with sandpaper. If I told them how I feel
they would start probing me for secret sins. I know I

---

*O God, you are my God, and I long for you. My
whole being desires You; like a dry, worn-out and
waterless land, my soul is thirsty for You.* Psalm
63:1

---

must have done something wrong, and I keep saying 'sorry', so why does God go on looking the other way? I want Him back desperately, but the more hassled I become, the farther He seems to recede.

I see from your book *Beyond Healing* that you had a similar experience so I thought you might understand. I just don't know anyone else who would. So on Sundays I put on my 'gleaming Christian face' and hope they won't realise I'm just a well disguised heap of rubbish.

Yours sincerely, Jill R

I put the letter down on the table beside me and sat gazing into space. I have known Jill for years and greatly admired the way she was always 'on fire' for God.

'Why should this happen to someone like her, Lord?' I whispered. 'Why does it happen to any of us?' I added ruefully. Once I, too, had thought no one else would understand, because no other Christian ever had the experience of losing God for no apparent reason.

Suddenly, in my memory I saw myself sitting at the dining table at a friend's house. My six, and her five children were making the baked beans on toast seem like the Lord Mayor's banquet. I had come a long way to see this friend because I was desperate and, like Jill, I had no wish to hang out my dirty washing in my local churchyard!

Before tea, while the children played in the garden I had tried to explain how I felt.

'When I was filled with God's Spirit, I thought my life would stay permanently full of joy, peace and power. I

> *Lord, why are you standing aloof and far away.*
> *Why do you hide when I need you the most?*
> Psalm 10:1, LB

didn't think I would ever be ill, or have money problems, and close contact with God would be a constant part of life.'

Earlier that same year I had been told by the consultant neurologist that the disease I had developed had permanently damaged my body, and was not only incurable, but it would probably keep recurring and sentence me to life in a wheelchair. I had smiled kindly at him, as I commented under my breath.

'That's what you think. It's *never* God's will for Christians to be ill.' When our minister had prayed for me in hospital I had expected to be healed instantly, but was quite happy to concede that God's healing might be gradual. What mattered to me far more during those long months in hospital was the new and intimate relationship with God that I was discovering.

On a flood tide of hope I had come home from hospital and plunged into the worst experience of my life. The more I believed I was getting better and tried to act as if I was, the more ill I became. Worse than that, I suddenly felt God had abandoned me. All the faith and joy that had sustained me over the previous months trickled away and was lost in the sand of a spiritual desert.

'Whatever did I do to bring this on myself?' I asked my friend. 'One thing after another keeps going wrong in our lives, so somehow I must have stepped outside God's protection. It just doesn't seem as if God's there any more.'

'Its a matter of faith dear,' she said gently. 'I *know* that,' I snapped crossly, 'but what are you supposed to do when your faith's all gone?'

Jesus answered him, 'You do not understand now what I am doing, but you will understand later.' John 13:7

Before she could answer, the children clattered in with roaring appetites and dirty knees, and soon we were all squashed round the table.

'Never mind, Jen,' soothed my friend, as she cleared away my plate of untouched food, 'just think how you will be able to use this experience to help other people one day.'

That remark was *the end*! The dam that I had so carefully constructed to contain my emotions burst violently.

'*How stupid!*' I thought, How could such a complete failure *ever* be used by God again? He had chucked me on the scrap heap like a rusty old car. I wanted so desperately to stay near Him, but I could not have felt further away if I had been Judas Iscariot. No! this humiliating experience could never be of use in any way. It was totally negative and destructive.

I could never have said all that, with eleven baked-bean-smeared faces gazing at me in astonishment. But the intensity of my feelings must have been obvious for I can still remember my friend pouring an apparently endless stream of tea all over her best table-cloth!

You are probably not supposed to write Christian books until you have all the answers tied up in neat bundles, but I could not wait for that. I began to write *Beyond Healing* as a kind of therapy and certainly, when it was finished, I saw my illness in a totally different light. But the thing that blessed me most was the mass of letters that followed its publication. From all over the world people wrote to say something like this;

What a relief, at long last to discover someone else who feels the same way as I do.

Where is the blessedness I knew when first I saw the Lord? / Where is the soul refreshing view of Jesus and His word? William Cowper

Jill was obviously only feeling a bit dry and spiritually 'switched off', while many other letters were from people who were going through much deeper and more painful experiences. Some were physically ill or depressed, while others grappled with unanswerable questions, such as 'Why did God allow my child to die?'

Soon the family began to dread breakfast-time when I opened the post and invariably dissolved into tears. Many of these people have become my friends – on paper – and I realise that one of the privileges God has given me is the time to communicate with them.

As I sat thinking how to answer Jill's letter that day, more than a year ago, I began to wonder just how many Christians there are like the two of us who hide their difficulties behind a smiling mask, while inwardly feeling like a modern leper without a bell.

Looking back over my life I could remember several bad patches, and I had thought I was the only 'unspiritual' Christian to experience that kind of thing. Was I wrong? Do other people also feel they ought to convey the impression that since their conversion or baptism in the Holy Spirit their lives have been one song of praise?

So I began to ask all my friends if they had ever felt separated from God, and after some initial reluctance I received a whole range of answers.

'Yes, I've had several patches when my Christian life felt rather dull and drab.'

'Twice I've had to go to my Bishop and tell him I suddenly could not believe a word I was preaching. He told me many clergymen go through patches like that.'

Thou wouldst not be seeking God, if thou hadst not already found Him. Pascal

'I seem prone to recurring bouts of depression during which I always feel God no longer loves me personally.'

Deserts are much more common than I thought

Soon I began to discover that these private feelings are shared by an astonishing number of other Christians.

'I'd like to write a book about these deserts,' I said as yet another letter fell in the marmalade, 'not just for people in them but also for their families and friends.'

Of course, I knew I could never do such a thing on my own. I am not a theologian; my only qualification is that I have been through several deserts and I know how much they hurt. So I plucked up enough courage to write to literally hundreds of Christians all over the world: clergymen, charismatic leaders, missionaries, doctors and scores of ordinary people like me. I asked them the following questions:

* Have you ever had a 'difficult patch' as a Christian?
* Do you know why?
* Did you gain anything from it?
* How did you escape?'
* Could you put me in touch with anyone else you know of who has been through the dark night of the soul?

I thought no one would bother to answer, but the letters came back like a freak wave, and many sent me several other names to follow up. 'It is such a relief to be able to tell someone how I really feel at long last,' was a recurring refrain.

Such is the nature of our trials that while they last we cannot see the end. Martin Luther

'Why,' asked one person, 'are we all so frightened to admit that our faith, joy and spiritual enthusiasm can sometimes flicker like a candle flame? Have we all been suppressing our feelings because "problems" are unfashionable these days?'

Some people hate writing letters so they talked to me on cassette, by phone or arrived in person on the door step. Soon I was in contact with over a thousand other Christians who were willing to allow me to draw on their experiences. My collection of letters and notes filled eight bulging files and provided me with a much clearer picture of what a spiritual desert is.

What a spiritual desert is
* A period of time during which a Christian's relationship with God becomes stale or strained.
* Difficult or tragic circumstances that make us feel God is angry with us or powerless to help.
* It can last from a few hours to several years. If we do not want to get out of it, it will last a lifetime.
* Deserts are felt very differently. For some sensitive people they are intense and devastating, while the easy going, placid types may find them a mere irritation.
* Sometimes the cause is obvious and easily put right, but the maddening part of many desert experiences is that at the time there is no apparent cause.

> *And don't tell me suffering ennobles people. I might punch you on the nose.* Wendy Green. From *Facing Bereavement* (Ann Warren, ed.)

The letters kept arriving

You might think that looking into over a thousand 'deserts' was a very depressing way to spend a year! Actually it was deeply exciting. My own faith in the sheer love of God has been strengthened enormously by hearing of the things people learnt about God *not* when they were being successful, prosperous and on a spiritual 'high', but when they had reached the end of their own faith, courage and even their desire to live. Letters like this:

Dear Jen,
Yes, I went into one of your deserts after my husband died, and it was pure hell. After the funeral I floated along on a cotton-wool cloud of other people's prayers. God was so close I used to think I would touch Him in the night if I reached out my hand in the darkness. But then suddenly, just when I needed Him most, He vanished.

One night in the bath I reached the depths of despair. As I lay there I suddenly thought, am I going to take God at face value or not? He said, 'I will never leave you; I will never abandon you.' (Hebrews 13:5) Either it was true, or He was a liar. Does He keep His promises or doesn't He? I asked myself, and amid the steam and soap I decided that definitely He does.

Just knowing that in my head, and setting my mind on it, regardless of feelings, has made all the difference and gradually my joy in Him has returned. Now I actually feel I am closer to God than I was before, something between us is stronger. Perhaps I've simply discovered that He really is always there, regardless of how I may *feel* at the time. That discovery was my

---

What we learn in the dark we possess for ever.
Edith Schaeffer

'treasure of darkness'. There's a verse in Isaiah (45:3) which says, 'I will give you the treasures from dark secret places; then you will know that I am the Lord, and that the God of Israel has called you by name.' Under the desert sands lie deep caverns and mines where we chisel out these gemstones, facts about God that we only discover at the darkest moments of our lives. They make us far richer when we come out of our deserts than we were before.

Much love, Mary.

No trite sayings

That letter might be irritating you if you happen to be going through a period of suffering. Perhaps you feel like my friend Dawn when she said:

> 'If one more person tells me, "We know that in all things God works for good with those who love Him", (Romans 8:28) I think I'll punch them! I don't want to be "done good to", I just want my son well again.'

These 'treasures of darkness' don't feel valuable at the time, more like lumps of hard rock. It is not until we are safely 'home' that we discover how 'rich' we have become. All the others who joined me in writing this book know what it is like to wait tensely for the next tactless remark made by someone who knows nothing about

> *I hate the darkness and fears that beset me, and I love high spirits, health, success and fun with friends, yet I have learned more in the darkness of unhappiness and pain than by hours of well being. Sufferings pass but what is learnt through suffering is treasure for ever more.* Leslie Weatherhead

suffering. The treasures of darkness we want to share are not sugary jingles or trite sayings. They are the priceless facts we discovered about God during the darkest times in our lives. Things that could only have been mined down there in the darkness.

2

THE BEGINNING OF THE END

Some wandered in the trackless desert and could not find their way . . . They were . . . thirsty and had given up all hope. Then, in their trouble they called to the Lord and He saved them from their distress. He led them by a straight road to a city where they could live. *Psalm 107:4–7*

It would be marvellous if from the experience of a thousand deserts I could offer you an instant formula for escape, an air ticket to 'green pastures'. But there is no easy way out. Those on the outside may say there is, but they are wrong!

Many people have discovered various escape routes, but they are only paths, not launching pads. You have to *walk* along a path, step by step, before it eventually takes you where you want to go. The first four steps of the journey are crucial. They are – realising where you are; wanting to escape; asking 'why?'; and seeking help.

The Lord said, 'I was ready to answer My people's prayers, but they did not pray, I was ready for them to find Me, but they did not even try.' Isaiah 65:1

1: REALISING WHERE YOU ARE

Most people drift into their deserts so gradually they do not realise what is happening.

'There was no dramatic turning away from God, He just faded slowly over the horizon,' was the way one person described it.

'I was sitting on the underground one morning,' said Malcolm, 'when a young man with a fish badge on his lapel sat down beside me. I felt irritated when he began talking about his faith. But after he got out, it suddenly struck me that I had once been as enthusiastic as he was. So excited about God, I even wanted to share Him with strangers in the rush hour. I had become so used to the boring routine of Christianity I'd been grinding along without thinking about it.

'For several days after that I would not admit to myself (or to God) that my Christian life was not what it had once been, or yet how I wished it could be. That weekend, I went for a long walk in the park and at last I realised I had been trying to kid the Lord for ages. That young man on the train had shown me how much I was actually missing the Lord. So I stopped by the duck pond and cried out to Him for help – silently of course! "Please get me out of this boring lethargy." It seemed to take months before anything really changed, but I would say the turning point in any desert is being honest with yourself and with God.'

In my alarm I said, 'I am cut off from Your sight!' Yet You heard my cry for mercy when I called to You for help. Psalm 31:22, NIV

Recognising where we are and asking for God's help are often the most difficult things to do in a desert, but they are also the most important.

'That's ridiculous,' you may be thinking, 'my main trouble is I can't believe He'll hear me.'

That does not matter, it is not our faith or lack of it that causes God to hear our voice. He is so eager to help He says,

'Before they call I will answer, while they are still speaking I will hear.' (Is. 65:24, NIV.) He'll hear you all right.

'But I'm far too ashamed to speak to God,' someone else might say. Sometimes we know we have walked into our wilderness deliberately and when we realise where we are, we feel we have forfeited our right to God's love. He seems millions of miles away and the steep, rocky path back to Him is too hard to attempt.

Someone once said that if you walk a thousand steps away from God, you only have to turn, and take one step back towards Him again, because He has followed you all the way. God does not wait until we have cleared up our lives, organised our relationships and changed our attitudes, He meets us just where we are, right at the very lowest point of our desert, and it is only God Himself who can help us climb back out of them again.

> *Though you have made me see troubles, many and bitter, you will restore my life again; from the depths of the earth you will again bring me up.*
> Psalm 71:20, NIV

2: DO YOU REALLY WANT TO GET OUT?

'Stupid question!' you may be thinking, but if we are honest, we have to admit that sometimes we are quite comfortable staying where we are.

David once said, 'I wish I had wings, like a dove, I would fly away and find rest . . . and live in the wilderness.' (Psalm 55:6–7) Deserts can actually become a refuge that we are reluctant to leave, an identity or even a way of life.

I am ashamed to say I quite enjoyed throwing 'pity parties' all round the district, rehearsing my many grievances to anyone who would listen. I wanted them to be as sorry for me as I was for myself! Sometimes we can almost feel proud of our deepest hurts and nurture them carefully because our problems are all we have left, and cuddling them close to our hearts can seem like a comfort. In the end that only makes us bitter, but we do not always recognise that at the time.

'If all my problems were solved,' said Karen to her house group leaders, after they had spent months counselling her, 'You wouldn't be interested in me any more.' Her desert had become her means of importance. We can actually *like* being the person they all pray for and ask round for meals. Remove the problems and our personality goes as well.

The desert can provide a good excuse
When we want to duck out of irksome responsibilities, we can use the desert as an excuse.

You will seek Me and find Me when you seek Me with all your heart. Jeremiah 29:13

'Oh well, if I've lost my faith I don't need to bother getting up for Church on Sunday, I'll have a nice sleep on, instead.'

'It would be hypocritical of me to lead that youth group now, so I'll resign. (Those boys were making my life a misery anyway.)'

There can also be a security in boredom
If we had to climb out of our rut we might feel exposed.

'Yes my Church does bore me to snoring point,' said Janice, 'my friend wants me to go to hers, but I'm not sure about this new kind of worship. What would people think if I started going there?'

It can take a lot of courage to walk out of a desert.

Has something else become more important to us than God?
It might be something wrong, but it could equally be very good in itself.

'We bought a boat, it was a great way to relax but soon we were off sailing most weekends, and we lost contact with our Church.'

'Once we had our baby we found it was difficult to get along to services and anyway we liked being a family together at home.'

'I put all my energy into running the Sunday School, and in the end that became more important to me than my relationship with God Himself.'

'We moved to an old house and doing it up ourselves took all our spare time.'

God wants us to live rich lives, full of relationships and activities. He simply asks that we share them all with Him and always put Him first in our lives.

The desert crisis

Robbie was the least likely candidate for a desert experience that I ever knew. Her love for the Lord had the same quality as that of the apostle John. Being single and nearly thirty-three did not seem to matter to her. The Lord filled her life, and the church music group was the pivot of her existence.

Then one day Keith joined the staff of the school where she worked. There always seemed so much to talk about during break, they both taught the same subject and shared so many interests. Soon it seemed logical to do their marking together and the staffroom was always so peaceful after school.

The evening that Keith told her how unhappily married he was, Robbie went into her desert. Oh, she did not recognise it for what it was, Satan saw to that. After all, she was doing nothing wrong, just talking to a lonely, misunderstood man, but church suddenly became boring.

Everything came to a head during a geography field trip. A week in the Brecon Beacons was like the daydreams she had enjoyed as a teenager. Their love was so enormous that they hardly noticed the two other teachers or their twenty sniggering pupils.

'I can't go back to Wendy after this,' whispered Keith, as they watched the sun set over Pen-y-fan on the last

> *Keep away from anything that might take God's place in your hearts*. 1 John 5:21, LB

night. 'I'm going to leave her. I'll have to find somewhere
else to live, I was wondering . . . if . . . could I move into
your flat?'

A few days later Robbie was playing her guitar in
church. The decision was still unmade and God did not
seem to be around to help her make it! There was
something very poignant about the music that day;
perhaps it would be the last time she would be part of it.
Church was *not* one of the interests she shared with Keith
and what would people think about them living
together? What would the Lord think?

That evening the sermon was about the Israelites coming out of the desert after their forty years of wandering
and how they crossed the river Jordan into their
Promised Land. During the closing prayer, Robbie saw a
vivid picture in her mind. God had often communicated
with her like that, but this was clearer than anything else
had ever been. She was standing on the desert bank of
the Jordan, covered with dust and her clothes encrusted
with sand. On the far side she could see Caanan, the fruit
trees on the sloping hills and the wild flowers in the
meadows. There stood Jesus Himself, His arms open
wide, His face twisted with longing as He called her over
the water to join Him. Everything inside her wanted to
leap forward, wade across the river and fling herself into
His arms for ever. Instead she looked back over her right
shoulder, back towards the dry, empty desert. There
stood Keith, silently beckoning her. The decision was
agonising. Like Lot's wife she stood on the bank, frozen
between two worlds.

Did she want to be out of her desert enough to say

> *Oh God, I don't love You, I don't even want to love
> You, but I want to want to love You!* St Teresa

goodbye to Keith and the companionship, security, even the children he could give her?

When the desert is at its most dangerous

There is, I believe, a crisis point in every desert when we have to make a decision either to cry out to God for help or to shrug our shoulders and think, What's the point of carrying on with Christianity when I don't get anything out of it any more? Perhaps I should take a break for a while, mustn't get too intense. This is the stage when the desert is *most dangerous*. Many people have thought, 'I can always go back to Christianity when I feel like it.' But Satan makes sure they never *do* feel like it, and one day they realise they have wasted years wandering aimlessly round an unproductive wasteland.

God is not like a half-knitted jumper you can put down and pick up again when you feel like it. He is a person, who said, 'My spirit will not always strive with man.' If we push Him to the back of a drawer He won't just lie there until we 'feel like' Him again. Perhaps this is one of the reasons why He allows us to feel far from Him – to see if we love Him enough to *mind* when we lose Him.

For months Robbie remained poised on the river-bank. Sometimes she would manage to 'give Keith up' and turn back towards Jesus, but then Keith would look at her across the staff room, or arrive on her doorstep late at night, and the old longing for him would return. She was stuck in this agonising situation when she came to speak to me.

If you hear God's voice today, do not be stubborn as your ancestors were when they rebelled against God . . . in the desert. Hebrews 3:7–8

'Change your job,' I urged her, 'sell your house, move away. Jesus said it was better for you to cut off a foot or a hand rather than allow yourself to be drawn away from Him.'

At that time Robbie was unwilling to take such drastic action, and as the weeks went by she actually wanted Keith more than she wanted her relationship with Jesus.

When we deliberately separate ourselves from God by a sin that we are enjoying, He minds terribly. But because He did not create us as robots, but gave us the privilege of free will, there is nothing He can do to help us out of our deserts if we do not want to leave them.

3: ASKING THE QUESTION 'WHY?'

'Why should this happen to me?' we bellow, when we feel God is far away. Jesus Himself cried from the cross, 'My God, *why* have you forsaken me?'

Satan likes to make us think deserts are always our own fault, and other Christians frequently do the job for him! However, just because there is often no instant answer to the question 'why?' does not mean we should not ask it. It is a fact that we do cause some deserts ourselves and sometimes there is a specific reason for our misery that we could easily put right if only we asked God to show it to us. My friend Amy assumed she knew the answer so she did not bother to put the question.

> *O Lord, Who art as the shadow of a great rock in a weary land, Who beholdest Thy weak creatures, weary of labour, weary of pleasure, weary of hope deferred, weary of self; in Thine abundant compassion, and unutterable tenderness, bring us, I pray Thee, unto Thy rest.* Christina G. Rossetti

'Ron took early retirement, and we moved down to the west country, bought an old house and took in three old ladies to help pay the bills. It sounded like a good idea back in Orpington, but it's been sheer murder. I'm on the go twenty-four hours a day. Ron has his golf, while I'm left holding the baby – or should I say three very bad tempered babies! I missed my old church terribly but had no time to join a new one. My spiritual side was gradually eroded by endless little jobs, until one day I realised I simply wasn't communicating with God any more. I thought it was overwork that was separating me from God, but as there was nothing I could do about that, I continued in my desert and became bitter and frustrated. I would have saved myself such a lot of hassle if only I had asked God 'why?'

One day when I was loading my ever-hungry washing machine I came to the end of myself and shouted,

'Lord, why don't you help me?' Nothing happened, but then a few days later Ron and I had a terrible row. We never row, we're not the type, but he was putting his golf clubs into the back of the car yet again and something inside me erupted,

'It was *your* idea to come down here, I never wanted to leave my friends. This is your pipe-dream, and yet off you go to golf yet again! Do you think I'm just your slave?'

I'd often thought all that, but never actually put my resentment into words, but as Ron drove away I

Answer me now Lord! I have lost all hope. Don't hide yourself from me . . . Remind me each morning of your constant love, for I put my trust in you.
Psalm 143:7–8

realised that even before we left Orpington I had been seething with suppressed anger.

I made a cup of tea and thought, 'That's the real reason for your problem with the Lord. It's anger and self-pity, not exhaustion at all.' Once I had confessed this to the Lord I felt close to Him again. Soon I found a lovely little church, and I cope with the ladies while Ron plays his golf. He stays in while I go to church. He was perfectly reasonable about it when I put it to him.

It would be marvellous if we could all escape from our deserts as easily as Amy!

Of course we all know sin separates us from God, so when He feels far away we need to pray, 'Lord have I done something to upset you?' God is more anxious than we are to remove anything that divides us from Him, so if we ask Him to identify the obstacle, He most certainly will.

There is no sin, however big, that can go on separating us from God, once we are willing to renounce it and go to Jesus for forgiveness. He took the blame and the punishment on the Cross. Deserts occur when we will not confess those sins.

All those months when Robbie was sleeping with Keith, she was telling herself, 'God understands, He knows we need each other.' She was trying to make herself believe *what she wanted to believe*.

You can change the hands of your clock to convince yourself that you are not late for work, but you cannot change the time. Neither can we bend God's rules to suit

Why am I so sad? Why am I so troubled? I will put my hope in God and once again I will praise Him.
Psalm 42:5

our own desires and expect to remain close to Him. He loves us to the uttermost, but He is a Holy God and it is impossible for Him to come near sin.

Robbie complained because she felt so far from the Lord, but He was simply showing His disapproval.

There is a story of a child who stole a large toffee and was caught sucking it by her mother. 'Jesus will be very sad you stole that,' she said sternly. The child burst into tears of contrition and her mother, fearing she had been too hard, said, 'Never mind dear, just say you're sorry, He'll forgive you.'

'I will,' replied the child, 'but not until I finish the toffee.' It is while we still want to go on sucking the toffee that we stay in our desert.

Deserts are never never a punishment for sin

When we finally want to regain our relationship with God, more than we want the 'obstacle' that is separating Him from us, we can be free instantly by asking God's forgiveness and turning away from that sin.

Satan hates that, so sometimes, *after* God has revealed the barrier of sin, and we have dealt with it, Satan still surrounds us with a vague cloud of guilt and worthlessness.

Mark allowed himself to be sucked into a dishonest business deal. For months afterwards he felt miles from God, but at last he went to his minister, confessed the whole sordid story and asked God to forgive him. Was

> *If we say that we have no sin, we deceive ourselves and there is no truth in us. But if we confess our sins to God He will keep His promise . . . He will forgive us our sins and purify us from all our wrongdoing.* 1 John 1:8–9

that the end of his desert? No, if anything it grew worse. Every time he went to church or tried to pray Satan would say,

'God may have forgiven you, but He won't ever want you near to Him again, not after all those filthy things you did. This feeling of isolation is your punishment.'

Satan was lying of course. Jesus died to take the punishment for Mark's sin, and after Mark had been forgiven, in God's eyes he was as innocent as if he had never sinned.

In desperation he went back to his minister. 'I just don't *feel* forgiven,' he explained.

'Suppose I handed you a cheque for a million pounds, just because I happen to be fond of you,' said the minister. 'You'd be a rich man wouldn't you?'

'Yes,' replied Mark.

'But the fact probably wouldn't sink in just at first – you wouldn't *feel* rich because you hadn't earned the money. So would that make the cheque worthless?'

'No,' smiled Mark, 'I'd take it straight to the bank.' The minister continued, 'God has forgiven you, that is a fact that your feelings can never alter. Jesus suffered instead of you, but I think you almost want to be punished because you cannot forgive yourself. You need to pick up this "cheque" that's lying here. Receive God's forgiveness and start enjoying it.'

That afternoon Mark walked out of his desert for good.

But because of our sins, He was wounded, beaten because of the evil we did . . . All of us were like sheep that were lost, each of us going his own way, but the Lord made the punishment fall on Him, the punishment all of us deserved.
Isaiah 53:5–6

Many deserts, however, are caused by enslaving habits and repeated defeat in the face of temptation. You will find more about these on page 97.

Sometimes the question 'why?' can become dangerous

Sometimes we may never know the reason why we had to go through a desert. When the missionary doctor Helen Roseveare was kidnapped and raped, God said to her later, 'Will you trust Me if I never tell you why?'

I believe, now, that repeatedly asking the question 'why?' actually hindered my escape. The main trouble with 'why?' is that it faces us in the wrong direction. You walk through a desert from one side to the other and you come out a richer person at the far end. If you keep looking backwards over your shoulder trying to see what caused you to be there, you cannot see the path that leads to freedom.

I did not realise we need only ask God once, on one specific occasion, then leave it to Him to send us the answer *if and when* it would help us to know. Every Christian acquaintance I turned to for help seemed to give me a different answer, until I was totally confused and that question 'why?' nearly drove me mad.

We must leave Him to answer in His time

If only I had stopped asking 'why?' and asked 'how?' instead. When you are lost in a geographical desert it

> *He does not punish us as we deserve or repay us according to our sins and wrongs . . . As far as the east is from the west so far does He remove our sins from us. Psalm 103:10–12*

does not matter in the slightest if you got there because your plane crashed, your jeep broke down or you fell off a camel. What does matter is *'how'* am I going to get out of this? And *'what'* treasure can I discover on the way?

'I will wait for the Lord, who is hiding his face . . . I will put my trust in Him.' (Isaiah 8:17)

4: SIGNALLING FOR HELP

When a person is stranded alone in the Sahara, survival depends on letting someone else know where they are. Any signal will do – smoke rings, a mirror perhaps, or even a radio.

Shouting for help is just as vital in a spiritual Sahara, but not nearly so easy! When we have always been the one to whom people come for advice, it takes a lot of courage to admit we are floundering ourselves. Many sensitive people, when they are suffering, like to crawl off alone into a hole, and even when we do manage to tell our friends how we feel they may not understand.

'The worst thing about spiritual deserts,' said one man who came to see me, 'is the hostility they arouse in other people.'

It has been tragic to hear about the ways other desert travellers have been hurt by their fellow Christians. It is not our enemies who injure us most, but our friends.

Job said, 'In trouble like this I need loyal friends – whether I've forsaken God or not. But you, my friends, you deceive me like streams that go dry when no rain

We don't know why we feel depressed, that's what's so depressing. David Watson comes.' (Job 6:14–17) Job desperately needed love and understanding in his illness and bereavement, and for a week his friends gave him just that, and then they turned on him. Our friends will also allow *us* a short excursion into our desert, and for a time we will be sustained by their love, attention and home-made sponge cakes.

Then, when their patience begins to wear thin we shall soon hear the familiar, trite remarks which feel like the sting of desert scorpions.

* Pull yourself together.
* You brought all this on yourself, you know.
* We all knew you were doing too much.
* You shouldn't be so negative.
* It's your own fault you aren't healed.
* You ought to read some books on 'triumphant living'.

Just a few days after Barbara's twenty-year-old son was killed on his motor bike, a 'friend' said to her,

'You must have allowed Satan in by some unconfessed sin.' The grief of losing her son was enough to bear without the guilt of perhaps having caused his death. That cruel remark plunged Barbara into three years of terrible depression.

'"Smile and the whole world smiles with you". That's true all right in churches. If you're full of joy you're full of friends, but if you're down people can't run away fast enough!' (Lesley)

> *Deserts isolate us, but perhaps we need these times of being outcasts in order to teach us to form our own opinion, rather than mindlessly following the crowd.* Gloria Moody

'I feel as if they've all ganged up on me, talking about me, discussing what I ought to do, judging me.' (Wendy)

'People come and listen to your problems but it's only to bolster up their own spiritual ego – "doing counselling". Afterwards they go off and ask people to pray, but it's only a pious form of gossiping.' (Jenny)

'I'm constantly having to endure long counselling sessions when amateur psychiatrists go tramping round my subconscious in hobnail boots.' (Stephen)

What is Satan up to in all this?

He is trying hard to isolate us from other Christians, because he knows we are more vulnerable when we are alone.

'I can always be with God in the woods and fields,' said my friend Gerry, when she felt people at church were criticising her. But God does not live in trees, He lives in people. That winter it snowed so heavily even the main roads were blocked. I was worried about Gerry whose cottage lay at the end of a lane, a couple of miles from the village where we were living. All she had were her chickens for company. So I put on my boots and floundered through the snowdrifts to see if she was all right.

'I'm fine,' she said, sticking her head out of the chicken house, 'and so are my hens.'

'Surely you don't leave them out there all night in these low temperatures,' I protested.

Is it nothing to you, all ye that pass by? Behold and see if there be any sorrow like unto my sorrow. Lamentations 1:12, AV

'They're all right,' she laughed, 'they all huddle up together to keep warm. Of course if you left one on its own it would be ready for the deep-freeze by morning!'

'Christians must be a bit like chickens,' I said later as I warmed my hands round a mug of china tea. 'We survive if we stay close to each other and share our heat; isolate ourselves, and we've had it!' Gerry understood what I meant, but she is still in the deep-freeze.

Christians can seem poor company when we are feeling 'out at elbows' with God, but strangely, we still need them. While it is both unwise and unnecessary to 'bare our souls' in public, somewhere in our circle of friends there will be one or two people who are wise and sensitive enough to understand us.

The one thing we need above everything else is prayer, especially when we are finding it hard to pray ourselves. It is imperative that we find some mature Christian who will pray for us. Someone really close to God to whom we can talk honestly, knowing they will neither pepper us with shallow advice nor gossip about our problems later. God will come to comfort us wearing their body, and speak to us using their voice.

Have you asked someone to pray for you?

Only eternity will show how much our generation owes to Billy Graham, but once he too had his desert experience.

'I prayed and prayed but the Heavens seemed to be

I kept quiet, not saying a word . . . but my suffering only grew worse and I was overcome with anxiety. The more I thought the more troubled I became. Psalm 39:2–3

brass. I felt as though God had disappeared and that I was all alone with my trial and burden. It was a dark night for my soul, so I wrote to my mother . . . and will never forget her reply. "Son, there are many times when God withdraws to test your faith, He wants you to trust Him in the darkness. Now son, reach up by faith in the fog and you will find that His hand will be there." In tears I knelt by my bed and experienced an overwhelming sense of God's presence.'

It was possibly not so much his mother's good advice, as her earnest prayers that rescued Billy from his desert.

Danger! Desert hazard
Don't let anyone make you feel guilty if during patches of severe stress or depression going to church is quite impossible (see Page 185). So long as you have that one Christian friend to pray for you and meet with you regularly, God can give you all you need until the worst pain is over.

Don't signal in the wrong direction
Some people, of course, do not withdraw into solitude when they are suffering. They go to the opposite extreme. Satan has to change his tactics with these extroverts because they automatically reach out towards people when they need help. So he tempts them to trust people too much.

I kept on believing even when I said, 'I am completely crushed', even when I was afraid and said, 'no one can be trusted'. Psalm 116:10–11

When our lives are full of problems, so often instead of praying, we dash round asking all our friends for advice. When everyone at Church has heard our story, we travel round the country in search of 'super stars' with a gift of healing.

Trusting people instead of God

When it is people we are trusting instead of God, the results are:

* confusion – they all tell us something different
* we are crushed by their condemnation
* our problems seem bigger every time we rehearse them
* we feel the church has let us down, so we leave
* and Satan has got his way.

Job said, 'Have pity upon me, have pity upon me O ye my friends; for the hand of God hath touched me.' (Job 19:21) If it is only the sympathy of *people* we want, we shall be disappointed as soon as he was.

The Lord says, 'I will condemn the person who turns away from Me and puts his trust in man . . . He is like a bush in the desert, which grows in the dry wilderness, on salty ground where nothing else grows . . . But I will bless the person who puts his trust in Me. He is like a tree growing near a stream and sending out roots to the water.' (Jeremiah 17:5–8)

> *God never fades from the vision of a person until he ceases to pray.* Oral Roberts

However well trained, famous or gifted people may be, they *themselves* will never get us out of our desert. God can only use people to help us when we first turn to Him in an act of the will.

Treasure of darkness

When Marion came to see me, the muscles of her neck and face were so taut she could not have smiled if she tried. Orphaned as a child, rejected by the man she loved, she had just lost her home and was finding her job in a Christian organisation an impossible strain.

'I don't want any advice,' she said hastily, 'I've been positively suffocated by tons of it. Now I've reached a point where people don't exist any more. I feel I'm standing naked and alone before God possessing nothing. I have been hurt so much in a way I feel I'm dead. Everything in life is lost now except my relationship with God. It's funny really,' she added with a stiff attempt at a smile, 'but actually all I've ever wanted in life was God, and now He is literally all I *have*.'

Marion had been basing her faith and Christianity on the people around her and they let her down badly. Yet, perhaps she had just made the most important discovery of her life – her Treasure of Darkness.

Let thy discontents be thy secret, if the world knew them t'will despise thee and increase them.
Benjamin Franklin

It seems ironic that Satan had tried so hard to crush her by the condemnation of others and yet, he had only managed to remove all her earthly props, pushing her right into the arms of God!

> *What else have I in heaven but You? Since I have You, what else could I want on earth? . . . God is my strength; He is all I ever need.* Psalm 73:25–26

3

IN THE DESERT YOU ARE A VIP

Jesus said: 'I have told you all this so that you will
have peace . . . Here on earth you will have many
trials and sorrows, but take courage! I have overcome the world.' *John 16:33*

Just suppose your desert story began as Job's did, with
God sitting in Heaven smiling down on you with pride.
(See Job 1:8)

'*There's* someone who really loves Me,' murmurs God
happily and all the angels smile agreement. 'Just look at
him worshipping Me there in church, and trying to
please Me in every detail of his life.'

Satan is also watching you with his crafty eyes just as
he once watched Job. The way that you love God and His
obvious pleasure in you irritates Satan into action. (See
Job 1:9–11)

'He only loves you for what he gets out of You,' he
begins. 'Look at him – healthy – attractive personality –
happily married – comfortably off, he only has to pray
and You do anything he wants. Is it any wonder he's
constantly full of joy and peace! You lavish Your power
on his ministry, and give him success in every project.
He's no fool, he knows he's on to a good thing! But . . .
just suppose You let me take everything away from him
would he *still* love You *then*?'

God hesitates. Why?

* Because He loves you so much He hates to think of you suffering in any way.
* Because of the risk. Satan might be right, a desert could cause you to reject Him for ever.

But God is prepared to take that risk . . .

* Because He knows this desert could bless you out of all recognition. He wants to add all kinds of new dimensions to your personality, and give you a deeper sympathy and understanding for other people, but He knows you can only gain these in a desert.
* Because He knows about the weak place that constantly defeats you, (impatience, selfishness, pride and so on.) He understands how much you long to be rid of these things but again He realises they can be eradicated only through adversity.
* Because He has mountains of riches stacked up for you in Heaven, and he wants you to look forward to them instead of being so preoccupied with the few grubby possessions you value down here.
* Because He wants you to love Him in the same way that He loves you. Not with selfish conditional cupboard love, but for Himself alone.

So, because God loves you enough to want only your best and highest good, and *not* to score points off his

---

Dear friends, don't be bewildered or surprised when you go through the fiery trials ahead, for this is no strange unusual thing that is going to happen to you. 1 Peter 4:12

enemy, or play spiteful games with you, He gives His consent and your desert begins.

Satan is powerless

Some people get so frightened of Satan they imagine him hiding behind every desert cactus. He is *completely powerless* to harm you in any way unless God first gives His permission, and God would never allow anything that was not ultimately for your total benefit. He knows you through and through and he will never allow Satan to send more than you can take. (See 1 Corinthians 10:13)

'If God is for us, who can be against us?' (Romans 8:31)

Satan sits in hell working out his strategy

These are his objectives:

* To make you doubt God's love, and His ability and desire to help you, even His very existence.
* To make you think that your life is no longer in God's control because you or your parents sinned and stepped out of His protection.
* To make you feel sorry for yourself, resent God and complain about Him, turn to other people or things for comfort and finally to reject Him altogether.

How will he achieve all this?

It is not only the dramatic events of life that Satan tries to

---

It may now be necessary for you to be sad for a while because of the many kinds of trials you suffer. Their purpose is to prove your faith is genuine. 1 Peter 1:6–7

use to separate us from God, he is just as active in the boring patches when nothing seems to be happening at all. He can use prosperity, success and ease. He knows when everything in our lives is going perfectly, including our Christian work, we don't need God at all. He tried to crush Job by adversity and failed but he managed to corrupt Solomon by wealth and fame.

The first battle

Satan didn't do too well with Job – at first. When he was ruined financially and lost his ten children in a mass tragedy, he said,

'The Lord gave, the Lord has taken away, may His name be praised!' Satan must have been livid. Perhaps you too won the first battle. You turned *towards* God when your life collapsed round your ears. But Satan tried again – he always does. Soon Job was desperately ill, rejected by his community and even his own wife. Still he managed to say;

'When God sends us something good we welcome it, how can we complain when he sends us trouble?' Job 2:10

The second battle went to Job too, but Satan waited, knowing he held the trump card. The devastating effect of 'long-suffering'.

When our Church is watching us anxiously, cheering us on and admiring how well we are coping with our illness or bereavement, we manage wonderfully. However, as the months go by, everyone drifts back to their own lives again and no one notices us any more.

The fruit of the Spirit is . . . long-suffering. Galatians 5:22. *Anyone can suffer 'short', it takes a lot more guts to 'suffer long'.* Tom Rees

Then our suffering can seem endless, cruel and devoid of reason.

Satan can wait, time means nothing to him. When it is eighteen months since the funeral and people feel we should 'be over it by now'. Or when you *still* have not found a job after two years. When the doctors have done all they can, and say 'you've just got to live with it'. That is when Satan's time really comes. Job did not manage at all well then. He said; 'I was living in peace but God took me by the throat and battered me and crushed me . . . He wounds me again and again he attacks like a soldier gone mad with hate.' (Job 16:12–14)

Satan must have grinned when he heard all that. Job never knew Satan was behind all his misery, he blamed God and his friends blamed him! No one thought of Satan. We and our friends still act the same and Satan loves it.

You are the VIP

You may feel totally alone in your desert, but you are watched by a countless number of beings. How you react *now* is important, not only to you, but also to them! You may feel your life is wasted and useless, but actually you are a vital part of the battle between light and darkness, good and evil.

We decide who wins

We are not just pawns in a huge game of chess played by God against Satan. Chessmen have no power, they go

> *Every battle of faith counts in God's sight, even if there is little or no victory to be seen at the time.*
> Sister Basilea Schlink

where they are placed. Although God and Satan are watching us more closely than any chess champions, *we* decide who wins.

When we wake in the morning and face another endless pain-filled day, the pointlessness of it all makes us wish we had died in the night. Actually, each day is a challenge. We are not just a forgotten grain of desert sand, God and Heaven care intensely how we are going to manage the day. If we walk through it clinging to God regardless of whether we can feel His presence or receive His blessings, His face will shine with joy and Satan will scowl in defeat. We will not see it, but it will happen. If we whine, grumble or shake an angry fist at God and turn for comfort or help to some other 'god', his face will twist with pain and Satan will smirk in triumph.

Poor old Job said a lot of things he regretted later (see Job 42:3). But while Satan may have won several battles he did not win the war and by the end of his experience Job knew God in a new and deeper way, and said to Him, 'In the past I knew only what others had told me, but now I have seen You with my own eyes.' (Job 42:5).

The ultimate prize for this war in the desert is your relationship with God. That is what Satan is attacking. Just how important is that relationship to you? Is it worth fighting for over a lengthy period? Or is it so trivial you will chuck it away when the going seems tough? We may not always win every one of those daily skirmishes but a failure should never discourage us; it is the whole war we want to win. We must never forget:

It isn't the days of high tension that try us most, and so give us most, it's the days that seem all grey and dull, they test the quality of the gold. Amy Carmichael, *Candles in the Dark*

* Abraham lied
* Jacob cheated
* Moses murdered
* Elijah ran away
* David committed adultery
* Peter denied Jesus

They all lost a few battles too. Jesus says to them and to all desert travellers who keep on going to the end, 'To those who win the victory I will give the right to sit beside Me on My throne, just as I have been victorious and now sit by My Father on His throne.' (Revelation 3:21)

Our prize is eternal, but not instant, and I know from bitter experience that deserts hurt! Let us never forget that God is not only up there, looking down on us, but also beside us, fighting with us on our side.

'When through fiery trials thy pathway shall lie,
His grace all-sufficient shall be thy supply,
The flame shall not hurt thee, His only design
Thy dross to consume and thy gold to refine.

'The soul that on Jesus has leaned for repose
He will not, He cannot desert to its foes;
That soul, though all hell should endeavour to shake,
He never will leave, He will never forsake.'

Richard Keen, *How firm a foundation*. From *Hymns of Faith*

4

BEDROCK FACTS FOR DESERT SURVIVAL

The people . . . said, 'The Lord has abandoned us!
He has forgotten us.' So the Lord answers, 'Can a
woman forget her own baby, and not love the child
she bore? Even if a mother should forget her child,
I will never forget you . . . I have written your name
on the palms of My hands.' *Isaiah 49:14–16*

The worst part of travelling through a desert is the
endlessly shifting sand. When you want to camp for the
night there is nothing firm into which to drive the tent
pegs. Our survival depends on discovering firm, hard
ground on which to base our existence – the bedrock
facts.

1: GOD NEVER LEAVES US,
HOWEVER WE MAY FEEL

My friend Jane looked distraught when she came to see
me in her desert.

'When something goes wrong,' she said, 'my immedi-
ate instinct is always to go to church to be there, in God's
presence. But when I went last week it was torture
observing other people finding the joy and comfort that
has been denied to me for so long. At the end I tried to
express to someone how I felt, and she simply said "If
God seems far away, guess who's moved!" But I haven't

moved. I'm running towards God as fast as I can. He's the one who's slammed the door in *my* face, why can't anyone understand that?'

The one thing a desert does to all of us is to make us feel God is far away, but that is never, never true.

Does the sun go away?

A few years ago we decided to try the Lake District for our holiday, because everyone kept telling us how beautiful it was there. Two wet, miserable weeks later we drove home again, sneezing all the way. Mountains? Were there any? All we had seen were gloomy clouds hanging low over our heads. Lakes? The lashing rain obscured them. Views? We had seen nothing but misted car windows.

'The sun must've gone to Africa, ' my smallest son remarked crossly as we sped down the motorway.

'Don't be silly,' his knowledgeable elder sister replied. 'The sun is always up there shining.'

'If it *had* been I wouldn't have felt so cold,' snapped Richard.

'You just have to *know* it's there even when you can't feel it,' said Naomi with finality. She was right and the same principle applies to God.

> I believe in the sun, even when it is not shining
> I believe in love even when I cannot feel it
> I believe in God even when He is silent.

Wherever God's children are – as they are still upon their Father's ground – so they are still under their Father's eye and care. They may lose themselves in a wilderness, but God has not lost them.
Matthew Henry

Those words were scrawled on the walls of a dungeon in
Cologne by a Jewish prisoner during the war. Where was
God when he wrote that? There in the prison with him.
Where was the sun when we shivered in the car park at
the bottom of Helvellyn? Shining brilliantly behind the
obscuring clouds. Where was God when I stumbled
blindly along in my desert? Right there beside me.

How do we know God is with us?

God said He would never leave us over and over again
throughout the Bible. 1 Samuel 12:22 says, 'The LORD
has made a solemn promise and He will not abandon
you.' God never breaks promises, He *is* close to us
whether we feel it or not.

'The best things in life are appreciated most after they
have been lost,' says Roy Smith. Perhaps it is possible to
take God for granted, just because He is always there. We
do not think about oxygen, we just breathe it automatically. Stand on the moon without an oxygen mask and
we would think of nothing else. Perhaps deserts make us
more aware of God than ever before.

Of course there are many reasons why we feel God has
left us and we will look at them later in the book, but I
wonder if the main purpose of a desert is not to give us
the chance to discover whether our feelings are actually
more important to us than God Himself.

These days we lay great emphasis on finding inner
healing, releasing ourselves in worship, gaining power
for our ministry and acquiring spiritual gifts to make our

Jesus said: 'I will be with you always'. (Matt.
28:20) *He promised us that we would always
have His presence, but He never promised that
we would always* feel *His presence.* Jean Rees

devotional life more fulfilling. As R. T. Kendall says, 'We are living in a "what's in it for me?" generation.' Perhaps we have lost that simple, ardent desire for God Himself, without all the trappings. The desert often robs us of the enjoyable side of our Christianity, even the 'fizz and bubble' of feeling close to God. Could the desert actually force us to ask if it is God we really want, or just the 'perks'?

If we can go on loving, obeying and putting Him first even when we are no longer getting anything out of it for ourselves we are actually beginning to love Him in the way that He loves us – totally unselfishly. 'For our life is a matter of faith, not of sight (feelings).' 2 Corinthians 5:7.

2: GOD MINDS ABOUT OUR DESERT

'I had this mental picture of God standing with His arms folded while I was sucked down in quicksands,' wrote Emma. 'If He cared about all I was going through, He would have done something to stop it.'

I remember feeling that God is so big and important, He could not possibly be interested in my affairs.

'It's all very well for you, Lord, sitting up there in comfort,' I remember muttering one day, 'Leaving me alone in all this pain.' The next morning I was reading my Bible (very unenthusiastically) when this verse 'hit me in the eye'. 'In all their distress, He too was distressed.' (Is. 63:9 NIV) Suddenly I realised that because He loved me so much, naturally He would mind terribly if I was

---

> *God Himself has said, 'I will never, never let go your hand; I will never, never forsake you.'*
> Hebrews 13:5. Weymouth

suffering, just as I would care if someone I loved was in pain.

God suffers much more in our deserts than we do

Just before I began to think about this book, the encephalitis flared up again and I was rapidly admitted to the hospital's intensive care unit.

I can remember little about it. I had such a headache I wanted to die, as I lay there gasping into my oxygen mask with tubes and needles protruding from every part of my body.

I do, however, remember feeling extremely sorry for myself, until I opened my eyes and saw my husband Tony sitting by my bed. The look on his face cured my self-pity.

'This is bad for me, but it's a thousand times worse for him,' I thought.

Why was it worse for Tony? Because he loves me and it is always much worse to watch someone you love suffering than it is to suffer yourself.

Why did Jesus cry?

When her beloved brother Lazarus became ill, Mary didn't worry, she knew Jesus. He even healed beggars so certainly He would use His power to save one of his best friends. She and Martha sent a message to Jesus and received this encouraging reply.

'The final result of this illness will not be the death of Lazarus.' (John 11:4)

Mary felt quite happy after that – until Lazarus died.

Thou canst not shrink from pain more than He dislikes thy bearing it. Cardinal J. H. Newman

Then she began to feel uneasy. Why had Jesus not bothered to come?

'He's probably on His way,' she comforted herself, 'after all He's raised the dead before now.'

It was not until after the funeral that Mary finally plunged into her desert. Jesus had let her down, even He could not raise a decomposing corpse. For four days she sat in a state of despair – then Jesus arrived. Martha dashed out to meet Him, but Mary stayed in her house. Was she too angry with Jesus to face Him?

'If He'd been here Lazarus would not have died,' she kept thinking, 'He doesn't really care after all.'

Many of us went into our deserts because we were totally bewildered by suffering. God did not answer our anguished prayers. The promises He appeared to give us became a hollow mockery. In our hurt and disillusionment we turned away from the comfort Jesus would have given us. If only we had got up, like Martha, and hurried out to meet Him.

Yet Jesus understood how Mary was feeling and He cared so much He sent Martha in to fetch her.

When Mary saw Jesus she told Him exactly what she thought of Him and then burst into tears. What did Jesus do? He wept. He did not cry for his friend Lazarus, He knew He was going to raise him from the dead at any moment. He wept for Mary in her agony of soul. He minded for her. He cries like that for us too, because He loves us just as much as he loved Mary.

He (God) found them wandering through the desert, a desolate, wind-swept wilderness. He protected them and cared for them, as He would protect Himself. Deuteronomy 32:10

How does God feel about the mildly drab patches?

God does not only grieve over us in our dramatic deserts, He misses our company during our 'dull times'. The story about Mary and Martha in Luke 10:38–41 proves that more than anything else He wants our company. So when we give up the habit of prayer and close our Bibles with a sigh of boredom because we feel cut off from God, it is actually God who is feeling cut off from *us*!

3: IT DOES NOT MATTER IF YOU HAVE LOST YOUR FAITH

One evening just before Christmas, Ann went over to her baby's carrycot to see if he was ready for his six o'clock feed and suddenly the world stopped. Andrew was dead.

'I remember reaching out towards God even before I screamed for my husband,' she told me. 'The doctor, police and friends came and went all that evening, but they were far less real to me than God, it was as if He was carrying me. At last, when I went up to lie down on my bed He allowed me to see right into Heaven and there was Andrew very much alive and completely happy.

He has an especial tenderness of love towards thee for that thou art in the dark and hast no light, and His heart is glad when thou dost arise and say, 'I will go to my father'. For He sees thee through all the gloom through which thou canst not see Him. George Macdonald

'That vision made life possible through the next few months – they were difficult, but I was coping. Then one day I was sitting by the fire, and suddenly a veil seemed to slip from my eyes. There was no such person as God, everything I'd believed all my life was a hoax invented by people to keep us happy. But I knew I was no longer deceived.

'It was rather a relief at first, no more struggling to understand God and His mysterious ways. Then as I sat there I began to feel icy cold. If there was no God then there was no Heaven, if there was no Heaven, my baby was dead and I would never see him again. If life finished at the grave then this precarious, unfair world was simply pointless. In a panic I realised my security had gone, without God who was there to turn to? I searched my mind desperately but it was as if my brain had clicked into a new programme of thought and I saw things from a totally different point of view. However hard I tried, I just could not believe anything the Bible said.

'As the days went by my Christian friends seemed like deluded fools. How could I go to them for help? But I had to talk to someone, so at last I made an appointment with our vicar and shaking like a leaf I sat down in his study. I thought he would be profoundly shocked when I told him my faith had gone – after all, I was the church youth leader. Instead he said gently. "I know how this feels, I've been through similar experi-

---

Even when we are too weak to have any faith left, He remains faithful to us and will help us, for He cannot disown us who are part of Himself and He will always carry out His promises to us. 2 Timothy 2:13, LB

ences, a great many Christians have. This is a very normal and common reaction to shock. Bereavement affects us like a physical wound, and you have to give wounds time to heal."

'He was right too. My faith did not return immediately but I was content after that go on acting as a Christian outwardly while I waited for my faith to return.'

This loss of faith is a ghastly part of many deserts. Sometimes, it happens suddenly, 'like someone switching the light off in your brain and leaving you in total darkness'. Others feel something like Pauline:

I kept having flashes of doubt. I suppressed them, but they kept on happening until I felt all tensed up and edgy.

After Ann's interview with her vicar she was 'content to wait'. She was in fact exercising the faith she thought she had lost. Faith is simply a willingness to wait. We do not bother to wait for a bus unless we know one is due. Faith means standing at the bus stop: you don't need faith when the bus arrives.

That God exists does not depend on our belief
One Easter Sunday my brother Justyn suddenly realised he did not believe a word he was preaching. His complete loss of faith persisted for well over a year.

> *It is not my grasp of God that matters most, but His grasp of me. The thing that matters most is not even my consciousness that He holds me fast, but just the blessed fact of it.* Francis James.

'I was *paid* to have faith and impart it to others,' he told me, 'so I felt I had to work hard to get it back. I sweated and struggled and spent sleepless nights pacing the floor or reading through mountains of theological books on faith!

'Then someone told me to relax and rest in the fact that God believed in me even if I did not believe in Him. My belief or lack of belief made no difference whatsoever to the fact that God exists and He loves me. Now when I meet other Christians who are hammered by doubts I tell them this;

* God chose you before you were born. (Jeremiah 1:5)
* While you were still a sinner Christ died for you. (Romans 5:8)
* He called you before you chose Him. (John 15:16)
* He loves you with an everlasting love. (Jeremiah 31:3)
* Nothing you do will ever make Him love you any less.
* Nothing you do will ever make Him love you any more.

Whether you believe does not alter the fact

'Of course,' continued Justyn, 'for a Christian to doubt God is a sin and when I realised that, I had to repent. Even now, years later, those doubts sometimes return fleetingly, but I'm ready for them now, and I repent at once and turn to the Lord for help before they have the chance to take hold of me again.

If from sheer physical weakness or from any other cause, you find faith faltering or failing, turn away from yourself and cling to this. God isn't faltering or even altering, 'He abideth faithful'. Canon Guy H. King

'What always helps me most is to remember Peter. When he stepped out of the boat he had so much faith he could even walk on the water. Yet, when he lost his faith he was actually much safer, because at that moment the Lord reached out and grabbed him. His safety did not depend on his faith, but on Jesus and so does mine.

'People have too much faith in faith. It is God Himself we need to trust.'

Do you want to have faith?

Once a man brought his handicapped child to Jesus for healing (Mark 9:14–29). Jesus said,

'Everything is possible for him who believes.' The poor man was devastated. He wanted to believe yet he felt he was letting his son down because his faith was not great enough to meet this challenge. When my baby son Duncan was ill I felt like that man. 'If he dies,' I thought, 'it will be my fault because I can't work up enough faith to save him.' When I explained my feelings to our vicar he said gently, 'It is not your faith that counts, but God's faithfulness.'

As that worried father stood before Jesus the tears ran down his face as he exclaimed,

'I do have faith, but not enough. Help me to have more!' For Jesus it was enough that the man *wanted* faith. He healed the boy at once and He did just the same thing for my son Duncan.

But what if some of them were not faithful? Does this mean that God will not be faithful? Certainly not! Romans 3:3–4

How do we cope when our faith has deserted us?
How do we operate while we wait for faith to return?
Matthew Chapter 28 verses 17–18 gives us the answer.
'They worshipped Him, even though some doubted.
Jesus drew near . . .' We need to keep ourselves in the
company of people who are not doubting, even when our
faith has gone. It is while we keep on worshipping with
them that Jesus 'draws near' to us again.

4: GOD IS BIG ENOUGH TO COPE
WITH OUR ANGER

The Lord is good, when trouble comes He is the
place to go! *Nahum 1:7*

It surprises me sometimes, that the files containing all my
'desert letters' do not actually burst into flames. So many
of them smoulder with rage. Deserts are full of very
angry people:

> *I prayed for faith, and thought that someday faith
> would come down and strike me like lightning
> from Heaven. But faith did not seem to come. One
> day I read in Romans 10:17, 'Faith comes by
> hearing and hearing by the word of God.' I had,
> up to that time closed my Bible and prayed for
> faith, I now opened my Bible and began to study
> and faith has been growing ever since. D. L.
> Moody*

'I just couldn't stand the new vicar, he's such a silly
little man.'

'I'm sick of other Christians offering me gift-wrapped
answers when my world has fallen apart.'

The Bible tells us clearly
Many of us have every reason to be angry but, the Bible
tells us clearly to:

* 'Get rid of all these things: anger, passion and hateful
  feelings.' (Colossians 3:8)
* and to do so before the end of the day. (Ephesians
  4:26)

That is easier said than done! First we have to recognise
who is the real object of our anger. Perhaps it is not the
bald-headed vicar, but God Himself. Subconsciously we
are furious with Him for allowing the misery He could so
easily have prevented. Yet we dare not admit our feelings, even to ourselves. So we transfer our rage on to
other people or turn it inwards and lash ourselves with
remorse.

To suppress anger is positively dangerous. We must
express it, but dare we actually do that to God Almighty?

Many of the greatest men in the Bible were very angry
with God, and they dared to tell Him so.

'If you are going to treat me like this, take
pity on me and kill me, so that I won't have
to endure your cruelty any longer.'
That was Moses. (Numbers 11:15)

*The bad experiences of our lives can either make
us bitter or better.* David Watson

'It's too much,' he prayed 'Lord, take away my life,
I might as well be dead!'
That was Elijah. (1 Kings 19:4)

'Listen to my bitter complaint. Don't
condemn me God . . . Is it right for You
to be so cruel?' (Job 10:1–3)

'Are you going to do nothing and make us suffer
more than we can endure?'
That was Isaiah. (Isaiah 64:12)

'Don't you care that we are about to die?'
That was the disciples. (Mark 4:38)

Have you ever felt like that? Did you tell God how you
felt, or did you withdraw from Him and redirect your
anger towards others?

I have always found the most special part of parent-
hood is being able to comfort my children when they are
hurt. I used to keep a jar of sweets in the first-aid box
along with the plasters and antiseptic. But Richard, my
youngest son, never wanted my love when things went
wrong, because he always seemed to blame *me*!

I would see him from the kitchen window falling down
with a terrible bang, but by the time I had hurried out into
the garden, he was nowhere to be found. Sometimes he
would hide for ages, frightened to express the anger he
felt. I was always so relieved when at last his adrenalin
level was high enough, forcing him to 'break cover' and
hurl himself on me, punching, kicking and bellowing out

Spiritual distress is the heaviest cross and greatest burden that a just, holy, wise and good God sends His believers. Christian Sciver

his rage. He was so tiny and helpless and I loved him so much I didn't care at all, and I knew he had to dissipate his anger before he would let me comfort him. When the tornado had spent itself, he would give me a rather sheepish hug by way of saying sorry, and our comfortable relationship was restored.

I was reminded of Richard when Shirley told me about her desert.

> I waited until the house was empty one evening, and then I shut the windows tightly. I was furious with God, and I wanted to tell Him so – loudly. I banged the kitchen table until my knuckles hurt. 'You've let me down!' I stormed, *'You just aren't fair!'*
>
> I went on and on like that, until suddenly I was frightened. Scared of my own anger. Would God strike me dead? I felt as if I had been behaving like a tiny child, deprived of sweets, beating his fists against his father's chest. I collapsed on the kitchen chair, feeling desolate and empty. It was then that I felt literally enclosed by His arms, bathed by His reassurance. It was as if he said, 'I'm big enough to take your anger. I love you and I understand.'
>
> I sat there sobbing with relief as I asked Him to forgive me for doubting His love, and that really was the turning point in my desert.

As human beings we have to express our anger. God is the only person big enough not to be damaged by that, and He also loves us enough to absorb it. However, even God Himself can be hurt by:

For we beat upon His chest from within the circles of His arms. Susan Jenkins

Chronic, persistent anger

One of my children had a school friend who struck me as a very strange little boy. He must have been about nine I suppose. He was quiet and 'good' at school, but his father told me he was impossible at home. His mother, to whom he was devoted, had died some years earlier, but it was not grief that made Gavin so difficult – it was anger. His father had married again within the year and Gavin would not forgive him for putting another woman in his mother's place. He expressed his anger constantly, and made his father's life a misery. The marriage broke up in the end, no one could stand the strain, and the last I heard of Gavin he was in a home for maladjusted children. Gavin's father had only wanted to provide him with the love and care of a substitute mother. He was doing the best thing possible for his son, but Gavin destroyed his father's plans by chronic anger.

An outburst of anger is obviously scriptural and it certainly lowers the blood pressure, but a long-term attitude of anger and resentment is quite another thing.

We can hurt God intensely

When difficulties arose in John's building and decorating business he naturally took them to God, but when God appeared to do nothing to help, John became angry. One day he was struggling to paper a client's lounge. The pattern would not match and the paper refused to stick to the walls. For John this was the last straw.

> *How often they rebelled against Him in the desert, how many times they made Him sad! Again and again they put God to the test and brought pain to the Holy God of Israel.* Psalm 78:40–41

'You just can't love me Lord,' he burst out, 'if you did You'd help!'

That night, still furious, he went to his house group. He had to – he was the leader! Someone had a prophecy which simply said,

'I *do* love you, are not My hands and feet proof enough?' Bowed in the quiet room, John 'saw' the Lord clearly before him, showing His wounded hands and side as once he had showed Thomas.

'Jesus said nothing,' John told me, 'but the look of hurt and pain on His face was too much for me, I realised with terrible clarity that my attitude was causing Him real suffering.'

There is nothing which hurts more than to love some-one to the uttermost, and then to have that person reject your love completely. God could not possibly love each one of us more than He does, so when we continue in an attitude of sustained resentment, anger and rejection He hurts no less than we would, if the person we loved most did the same to us.

The most vital fact

The most vital bedrock fact of all is that God only wants to bless us, whatever we are going through, just as Gavin's father wanted to do the best for his son. Our attitude can hinder God's plans or cause them to materialise – it is up to us. God loves us so deeply that when we deliberately throw away our chance of His blessing, He *minds* for us.

So, whether we express our anger and bewilderment in a childhood 'temper tantrum' or smoulder away for

> *Let us return to the Lord! He has hurt us, but He will be sure to heal us; He has wounded us but He will bandage our wounds.* Hosea 6:1

many months, we need to follow the example of Job before our communion with God can be restored. He was perhaps more rude to God than any other person in the Bible, but at the very end of his book he says;

'So I am ashamed of all I have said and repent in dust and ashes . . .' Then the Lord made him prosperous again and gave him twice as much as he had had before. (Job 42)

5

THE DESERT CRISIS

In the shadow of Thy wings will I make my refuge until these calamities be overpast. Psalm 57:1, AV

Most people who have been through a desert look back on one particular incident which they remember as their desert crisis. They use different words to describe it, such as: 'Reaching the end of myself,' 'rock bottom', or 'my turning point', but they are all talking about the same thing. One person put it like this.

When my husband was seriously ill I went on like the perfect vicar's wife – said all the right things, and kept my smile pinned on firmly. But inside I was in a turmoil. I remember thinking, 'I'm hanging over a black hole. If I let go I'll hit the bottom and disintegrate'. So I just went on holding on to the edge by my finger nails, praying constantly that God would spare Peter's life.

One day another clergy wife sensed I was not really as 'all right' as I pretended to be. When I explained the 'black hole' feeling to her, she said, 'why don't you let yourself fall, dear, because when you do, you'll land right into the arms of Jesus. He's got this whole situation in His control.' I collapsed into a chair and burst into floods of tears. I realised I had not been trusting Him to care for me if Peter were to die. I had been resisting His love while I tried to cope by myself. I felt I was falling down and down and I tensed myself to feel the sharp rocks on the bottom, but 'underneath were the everlasting arms' and I have never felt so comforted in my life. (The eternal God is your refuge and dwelling place, and underneath are the everlasting arms. Deuteronomy 33:27)

The 'black hole': the crucial point

It is not the difficult circumstances of our lives that cause our spiritual deserts, but our reaction to them. The human instinct is usually to fight, to try and escape from an unpleasant situation as quickly as possible. Of course we should declare war on our problems – it is never right to lie down in a defeated, self-pitying heap. If you did that in the Sahara you would certainly die within hours! We should try to escape our desert by:

* Prayer perhaps with fasting.
* Seeking God's healing or deliverance.
* Confessing our sins and changing our attitudes.

Yet when we have done every single thing we can do, sometimes the situation does not change at all. It is then that we reach our crisis, the 'black hole'.

At the lowest point of every difficult situation stands Jesus with his arms open wide, longing to comfort us. He is saying, 'Will you give this to Me and trust Me to sort it out?'

If we know how much He loves us, we should always be ready to receive equally and with indifference from His hand the sweet and the bitter, all would please that came from Him.
Brother Lawrence

If we turn to Him at that point, our spiritual desert will probably be over, even if our human suffering may have to continue. But when we argue with God our desert is prolonged and our misery increases.

God only intended the Jews to take a few weeks to cross the Sinai Desert after He rescued them from Egyptian slavery. Yet He could not give them the Promised land until they had learnt to trust Him completely. It was their grumbling, complaining and rebellion that kept them in the desert for forty long years.

To accept a desert in all its bleakness, confusion, or grief can be the hardest thing God ever asks of us. When Jesus was in the Garden of Gethsemane He fought against the thought of the cross which lay ahead of Him and prayed until He sweated blood.

'Let this cup pass from Me.' He wanted that suffering removed, but He knew that His Father would never allow anything unless it would bring ultimate and long term good. So He bowed his head and accepted it. 'Nevertheless not My will, but Thine be done.' He could accept even the horror of the cross because He knew that all things work together for good to those that love God.

'All things' means deserts, too

It was because I did not realise that 'all things', means, good *and* bad things that it hurt me so much to be in my desert.

> God, grant me the serenity
> To accept the things I cannot change.
> The courage to change the things I can –
> And the wisdom to know the difference.
> B. Niebuhr

'This illness can't be God's will,' I thought. 'So what caused it?' For months I used every gram of my energy trying different ways to find healing until in the end I became so exhausted my physical condition grew worse.

'Satan's won!' I cried, when my friend Grace found me in tears one day.

'That's just what I thought,' she replied. 'When my husband left me with four kids, I just would not accept the situation for months, so I wrestled in prayer and beat on the doors of Heaven. "Lord, You've got to bring him back, I can't cope without him." I used to shout until I was quite worn out. But still my husband didn't come back.

'One day I found a tiny phrase from a poem written by the missionary, Amy Carmichael: "In acceptance lieth peace". Who was I to say what God should do? That was up to Him. I've gone on praying for a reconciliation ever since, but from that moment I nestled into God, and began to live again.'

'But Grace,' I argued, 'Acceptance is a cop out. *We must* fight bad situations or they drown us.' Grace smiled her crooked smile at me as she replied.

'When the waves are coming at us they will drown us if we just weakly let ourselves sink under them – that's resignation. But acceptance is a strong action: it means flinging ourselves on to the crest of the wave and allowing it to take us into the shore.'

After that conversation with Grace I still went on trying to manipulate God for months – all the way to my Black

---

Woe to the man who fights with His Creator. Does the pot argue with its maker? Does the clay dispute with him who forms it, saying, 'Stop, you're doing it wrong!' Isaiah 45:9

Hole! But eventually I too found that 'in acceptance lieth peace'. I also discovered that,

Door out of the desert
Acceptance is the door which leads out of the desert. Acceptance is an act of the will, a decision we make without the help of wonderful 'bubbly' sensations – we simply decide to take whatever God gives us, asking for His help *in it* and not by having it removed. When we accept a difficult situation God does not necessarily change it, though He might. What He *does* change is the way we feel about it.

Acceptance is not a 'one off' decision
Ruth and Goff's 'black hole' happened as they sat in the hospital intensive care unit beside their sixteen-year old daughter. That day at school, Barbara had suffered a massive brain haemorrhage.

'How we prayed,' they told me. 'We had no doubt in our minds that God would heal her, so we sat there praying away in tongues for hours, regardless of the nurses and doctors. Suddenly, at the same moment we both knew the Lord wanted us to trust Barbara to Him. He was the one who knew what was really best for her. As we held hands across her bed we gave our daughter to God, to do what He wanted, and we stopped demanding that He should do what we wanted. Complete peace seemed to settle round all three of us and a little while later the Lord took Barbara home to complete safety.'

God wants us to accept everything and anything with a smile, not with gritted teeth. Mother Teresa

'Did that feeling of peace remain with you?' I asked.

'We have always known that Barbara is in the safest place in the universe,' replied Goff. 'We've watched one of her school friends getting into trouble with the police, several others mixed up in drugs, and many more facing all kinds of unhappiness and danger and we often wonder just what it was that the Lord saved our Barbara *from*.'

'So you never had any problem with acceptance,' I pressed them.

'Well,' hesitated Ruth, 'Acceptance isn't something you just do once, it's a continuous struggle. I'll suddenly see a young mum pushing a pram and I'll think, "that could have been my Barbara". Then I have to give her to God all over again, right on the spot.'

It is never too late for acceptance

That story may be worrying someone whose reaction to suffering was not so immediately accepting as that of Barbara's parents. Perhaps that is why God allowed me to meet Jan, just a short while after they visited me.

She too, once sat next to her daughter in an intensive care unit, but she felt nothing but outrage when she saw so many children all around her suffering so cruelly.

'Under my breath I snarled, "Go away God, You cosmic sadist! Following you makes life too difficult." For nearly three years after that I felt a total absence of God, no church, no prayer, no hope. I thought God had taken me at my word and gone for good. As my husband and

---

Being able to acknowledge that He knows what He's doing in the midst of difficulty, that is a goal worth striving for, it is precious to Him when we trust Him through some difficulty. June Dickie

friends kept on praying for me, I slowly began to yearn for God again. Gradually I came to accept that our daughter will be permanently handicapped and at last I was free to recognise the good things in the situation.'

When we cannot forgive God

What is it that keeps us hanging over the edge of our 'black hole', unwilling to trust God and fall into his arms? I think it is that we cannot forgive God.

Of course He never engineers tragedies, but when God sees something is about to hurt us He could easily step in and stop it. But often He does not because He knows He can use it for our benefit. Satan, other people or we ourselves may have caused our misery, but it is God who takes the final responsibility. He is the supreme ruler of the universe. To say that He is powerless to protect us is to say He is less than God.

I used to think that it is always God's will for His children on earth to be whole physically and to live problem-free lives. I must have been wrong, because:

* There is not one Christian in all the world who is ever one hundred per cent healthy. Everyone has something that is imperfect.
* None of us goes through life without problems.
* We all die in the end.

So is God's will thwarted in us all the time? If it were, He would not be God. No, Jesus said we would have trouble in this life (see John 16:33), but in Heaven at His

---

Let us see God's hand in all events and let us see all events in God's hand. Matthew Henry

right hand are pleasures for evermore. (Cf. Psalm 16:11)
If God had intended us to be exempt from the natural
problems of all human beings He would have made us
into angels.

We need to forgive God even though He has done no wrong

'I could accept that I'm disabled more easily if I did not
believe in God's ability to heal me!' snapped Diana. The
day she was packing to leave for medical school she had
been involved in an accident which has left her crippled
and badly disfigured.

For three hours one morning she told me about all the
different people who were to blame for the accident.

'Even the surgeon removed more of my damaged brain
than he should,' she finished angrily.

'But God could have prevented the whole thing.' I put
in quietly. 'Do you believe that?'

'Oh yes,' she said impatiently. 'I even remember
praying for safety as I got up that morning!'

'Then surely it is God who takes the final responsibility
for the accident. If a human being causes us pain, grief or
hardship our relationship is broken until we forgive
them. If I chanced to be standing behind the door when
Tony suddenly opened it, I would probably be furious
with him for my bleeding nose and headache. In my hurt

---

*He has not created me for naught. Therefore I will
trust him. Whatever, wherever I am . . . He does
nothing in vain. He knows what He is about. He
may take away my friends . . . make my spirits
sink, hide my future from me, still He knows what
He is about.* Cardinal Henry Newman

and rage I might blame him, even though he had done me no wrong, he simply opened a door. I would have to forgive him before our relationship could be restored.'

Diana was looking at me with a growing expression of horror on her scarred face. So I hurried on to explain what I meant.

'There has to come a time when we say, "Lord, I forgive You. I know you have only allowed this for my ultimate good, but right now I am hurting – badly!"'

'Forgiving God!' gasped Diana, 'That's blasphemy!' and she swept out of my room and slammed the door. I spent a terrible few days feeling I had permanently destroyed her faith in the love of God, yet when I looked in my dictionary it said forgiveness means: 'ceasing to blame, giving up resentment against'. Could Diana ever manage to do that to God?

Two days later she was in my room again, a different girl.

'I did it,' she said quietly. 'I told God I forgave Him for not preventing the accident that day, and I asked His forgiveness for blaming Him.' Then she added with a sudden smile, 'and I said to Him, "I don't know what you're doing, but I know *You* know, and I trust You." Now there are no more nasty shadows between us.' Yes, as Amy Carmichael affirms, peace really does lie in acceptance!

Prosperity is the blessing of the Old Testament, and adversity is the blessing of the New Testament. Francis Bacon

6

THE 'BEFORE' AND 'AFTER' DESERTS

When He has tested me I shall come forth as gold.
Job 23:10

The huge marquee resounded with joy as thousands of people praised God unanimously. This was the last night of a great Bible Week, and many people had received a wonderful new blessing.

'Thank you for filling me with Your Spirit,' gasped Louise, 'Now I love You more now than anything or any one.'

'What's gone wrong?' demanded the same girl, eleven months later as she stormed into her vicar's study. 'I was on cloud nine after last summer. I thought I'd feel like that for ever, but now everything in my life keeps going wrong, and God's not doing anything about it. I'm beginning to wonder if that experience was phoney, just mass hysteria.'

The vicar tried to speak, but Louise continued without taking breath. 'I've read so many books which describe dark patches that people go through, but then they are baptised in the Holy Spirit and the books imply that all their troubles were over – "she married the prince and lived happily ever after". Why hasn't it worked out like that for me?'

'My dear,' commented her vicar at last, 'don't forget that God only tests those who are really precious to him.'

'In that case,' snapped Louise, 'I'd rather not be that precious!'

The new blessing that Louise had received at the Bible Week was real all right, more real than life itself. She was simply in:

The 'after' desert

So many deserts seem to happen *after* some great new blessing, *after* receiving a new spiritual gift, a revelation or vision for future service, even after a deeper personal commitment to God. Just when we feel we ought to march out in triumph to take the world for God by storm, we find ourselves floundering about in a desert.

Perhaps we feel as badly 'let down' as Louise, yet is this not exactly what happened to Jesus? He was baptised and heard God's voice speak to Him from heaven affirming that He was His own Son. Did He stride straight off to Jerusalem and start telling everyone He was the Messiah? No He was 'led of the spirit into the desert to be tested'. There Satan tried every way he knew to make Jesus doubt His deity and God's plan for His life.

All new things have to be tested. Before an aircraft is licensed to carry passengers it is subjected to tests of every kind and in an 'after' desert our 'new blessings' are being shaken and rattled like a VC 10 in a wind tunnel.

It is easy to love God in the blazing sunshine of a mountain top experience, but can we go on loving Him as we grope about in the dark valley which so often follows?

> *Though God doth visit my soul with never so blessed a discovery of Himself, yet I have found again and again that such hours have attended me afterwards that I have been in my spirit so filled with darkness that I could not so much as once conceive what comfort was with which I have been refreshed.* John Bunyan

As Louise sat facing her vicar she had to decide how important her new blessing really was to her. Would she cling on to it tenaciously, or shrug her shoulders and find something else to fill her life?

The dark night of the soul – God's test for love

Five hundred years ago a monk we now call St John of the Cross described deserts as 'The dark night of the soul' and he stated that they are God's way 'of purifying the soul of everything that hinders its close relationship with God and ability to serve Him'. Many Christians are quite content to jog along happily as solid church-goers with God in one department of their lives. Probably they will never be troubled by the 'dark night of the soul'. A smaller group of Christians want to love God with everything, not just a part. Their path will undoubtedly lead through deserts because God will have to discover if their love is pure of any taint of self-interest.

'Souls begin to enter into this dark night when God draws them out from being beginners,' says St John. A desert is a sign of Christian maturity, not of failure!

In the marquee Louise told Jesus she loved Him more than anything or anyone else. When the feeling of spiritual ecstasy died out of her Christian life Jesus was asking, as once He asked Peter, 'Louise do you love me more than these? More than the fun of meeting your friends in church? More than you enjoy My power to do supernatural things? More than the excitement of having your prayers answered?'

What is a religion worth which cost you nothing? What is a sense of God-worth which would be at your disposal? Frederich von Hügel

Of course God does not want our lives with Him to be a harsh grind, and in time He gave Louise back all her enjoyment but with an added depth. God wanted to be loved for Himself, and not just for his gifts. He wanted to be more important to Louise than the excitement of being a charismatic Christian.

After some great achievement for God

Many people told me that their desert came almost as a reaction;

'After I gave my testimony at our church carol service.'

'I worked so hard helping with our church mission that afterwards I felt a bit like Elijah after Mount Carmel!'

Martin Luther is remembered throughout history for his great trial at Worms, when he stood out against the power and corruption of Rome and launched the Reformation. Afterwards he was in such danger his powerful friends smuggled him away against his will and hid him in a lonely castle in the forest. For a year he was in a horrendous desert. All his life he struggled against frequent bouts of depression when he 'doubted that God is good and that He is good to me', but Luther's 'After Desert' was the worst he ever experienced.

As he lay on his damp bed unable to sleep, he would wonder if he had been right to say 'the just shall live by faith alone?' If he was wrong he would carry all his

Give me Thine own self, without Whom, though thou shouldest give me all that ever Thou hast made, yet could not my desires be satisfied. St Augustine

followers with him to hell. For a whole year he suffered mental agony, but when he eventually came out of hiding an eye witness described him as 'a man aflame with God, and twice the man he was before'.

The 'before' desert

When someone is plodding wearily through a desert the last thing to occur to them is that God may be preparing them for some great work. Yet from the Bible down through church history, few people of God have *not* gone through a desert before embarking on a great work for Him.

Jamie Buckingham describes the desert as 'a scorching crucible that has burned from proud men both sin and selfishness until they have emerged pure and prepared for ministry.'

'I have tested you in the fire of suffering.' (Isaiah 48:10)

God told Joseph he was destined for greatness through a dream when he was still a boy. But years of rejection, exile, slavery and imprisonment had to come before he was ready to be the world statesman God needed.

David was a 'rosy-faced' shepherd boy when God told him he would be king one day. First he had to endure years as a fugitive hiding in the desert from the jealousy of Saul.

Moses was a proud, headstrong prince who sensed his job in life was to free three million jews from slavery. But

> *Hardly any outstanding champion of faith who has left an indelible impress on man's spiritual life can anywhere be found who has not won his faith and confirmed it in the face of trouble.* Harry Fosdick

he thought he could do it his way, and landed himself in a real desert with murder on his conscience. After forty years contending with a few scrawny sheep and an unhappy marriage, the Bible describes him as the most humble man on earth. He was ready for God to use him to accomplish a major assignment.

I have never met anyone in a desert who can possibly believe God will ever use them again! I felt infuriated with my friend – the one who poured tea all over the table – when she tried to suggest that my desert might be a preparation for something God wanted me to do. Yet she was right. As I look back, I can see it was not the end of the road, but the beginning of the completely new and exciting life that God had planned for me.

Probably we could all accept our deserts far more easily if only we could see them in the context of our whole lives. The most trying part of spiritual deserts is that at the time we never realise their significance!

Never doubt in the dark what God said in the light.
Arne Peterson

A cricketer can never score runs unless he is bowled at. Tom Rees

7

THE DESERTS THEMSELVES

Now change your mind and attitude to God and turn to Him so He can cleanse away your sins and send you wonderful times of refreshment from the presence of the Lord. *Acts 3:19*, LB

1: THE DESERT WE CAUSE OURSELVES

In this chapter we are looking at the many things make us *feel* separated from God. The Bible tells us that the only thing that ever actually *does* separate us from Him is our own sin. There is one prayer which God always answers, 'Search me O God and know my heart. Point out anything you find in me that makes you sad.' (Ps. 139:23–24. LB). If your desert is caused by sin, God will certainly tell you. If you then ask His forgiveness and resolve to stop sinning in that way, *your sin is wiped out!*

The unforgivable sin

Of course Satan may try to blind you to the fact that you can be so instantly and easily free. I have met three people this year who thought their particular sin was unforgivable.

I was whizzing through the park in my electric wheel chair when I first met Tess and her black labrador. We both admired each other's dogs and half an hour later we were still talking!

'You must get very bored, being disabled,' she said. 'Whatever d'you do all day?'

'Actually I'm writing a book,' I replied, feeling rather silly. When she pressed me, I told her it was about people who feel separated from God.

'That's me,' she replied turning pale. 'I used to love going to church more than anything, but of course I had to stop when . . .'

'When what?' I asked her gently,

'When I realised I'd once committed the unforgivable sin,' Tess whispered miserably. 'Ten years ago I had an abortion. We already had two children and wanted to educate them privately, so it seemed sensible at the time, but I have never regretted anything so much in my life. Going to church was a great comfort, until I heard someone on television say that abortion is unforgivable to God.'

'The fact that you are *worried* you have committed the unforgivable sin, is a sure sign you haven't!' I told her. 'No sin is unforgivable if you are willing to ask God's forgiveness. If Hitler himself had been genuinely sorry for all he did, and turned to God in repentance, we would meet him in Heaven one day.'

Tess gazed at me and then she said,

'You really mean it's possible that I could be free of this?'

When I next met Tess I could see by her face that she was finally free of Satan's lie.

The mess that sin leaves behind

Another of Satan's ploys is to say, 'Look at the mess

Though I have fallen, I will rise, though I sit in darkness, the Lord will be my light. Micah 7:8

you've made of your life. What's the point of having your sins forgiven when you'll still be helplessly enmeshed in their consequences?' He loves to remind you that the decisions you made when you were temporarily 'off the rails' have left you stuck in a difficult situation from which you cannot now escape.

'The results of my mistake are a constant reminder of the wreck I've made of my life,' said a man I met recently. 'Now I can never be a first-class Christian – I've spoiled all the plans God made for me.'

God deals with our sins and their consequences

There is no such thing as a second-class Christian in God's eyes. When we are forgiven He sees us through Christ as if perfect. We may have surrounded ourselves with an ugly heap of rubbish which seems to trap and defeat us, but if we give it to Him, God will take delight in making something beautiful out of it.

Antique Eastern carpets were usually hand-knotted by apprentice boys. When the master carpet-maker came round to view their work he might discover a mistake they made days before. Yet he did not insist the whole carpet was thrown away, neither did he order hours of work to be unpicked. Because he was the designer, he simply incorporated the mistake into a new pattern, using it to create a unique effect.

'I look to the Lord for help at all times, and he rescues me from danger,' says David in Psalm 25 verse 15. If we keep concentrating on the Lord He will show us how to cope with our difficult situations, step by step. When

---

If God tells us to forgive seventy times seven, it stands to reason He will do even better Himself.
Thomas Bilney

David had confessed the sin of his adultery with Bath-sheba and the murder of her husband (Ps. 51) they later had a son, King Solomon, who was the wisest man who ever lived. David had many wives, yet it was through Bathsheba that Jesus descended. God made a very special carpet out of that situation!

The little sins that don't really matter

If Satan cannot crush us by making us feel our sins are too big for God, he will make us think they are too small to matter.

It is possible to be working happily for the Lord, full of joy and power when, suddenly, into our lives creeps something so small we do not even recognise it as sin. We begin to feel drab spiritually but perhaps we put it down to overwork. When our consciences begin to prick, we think, 'That's impossible, God would never bother about something as trivial as this.' Yet it is surprising just how many little things the Bible tells us will destroy our worship and prevent God from hearing our prayers. Because they are often things we enjoy we reason away to our consciences like this:

* Everyone else does it, it's our modern life style.
* God understands – He loves me and I've even prayed about it.
* We all have our little 'besetting sin'.
* Compared with other people round here, I'm a saint!

> *Let not small and trivial sins be despised. With little drops the river is filled. Through narrow chinks in the ship the water oozes into the hold and if it be disregarded the ship is sunk.* St Augustine

Satan either makes us think of God as a punishing tyrant or he gives us the equally false impression of a jovial Father Christmas, distributing endless presents. When we sin we imagine God smiles indulgently and pats us on the head. But if He could treat our sin like that why did Jesus have to die in agony? He did not suffer just for the sins we think are serious – adultery, robbery, murder. He died because all sins are the same size in God's eyes and they all separate us from Him.

Thoughts are as serious as actions

Outwardly Josie looked as if she was listening attentively to the sermon, but inwardly she was having sexual fantasies about the curate who was preaching. Josie would never dream of *doing* anything wrong, but Jesus tells us clearly in Matthew 5 that to *think* adultery is as serious in God's eyes as committing it outwardly. It is also as bad to feel bitterly angry and resentful towards another person as it is to commit murder!

Josie told herself that 'day dreaming' was all right because 'it didn't hurt anyone else'. But when she found it was interfering with her worship, she realised it was actually hurting both herself and God.

'But now I can't seem to stop. These thoughts just pop into my mind even when I don't want them and make me feel dirty,' she told me tearfully.

'Suppose a salesman knocked at your door,' I said, 'trying to sell something you can't possibly afford. You could say firmly, "No thank you", and shut the door. Or

---

The steps of a good man are directed by the Lord. He delights in each step they take. If they fall it isn't fatal, for the Lord holds them with His hand.
Psalm 37:23–4, LB

you might ask him into the sitting room, make him coffee and read all his brochures.'

'If I did that,' smiled Josie, 'I'd probably find myself lumbered with his product!'

'Satan shoots darts into our minds constantly,' I continued, 'a lustful thought, a sudden surge of resentment, self-pity, a flash of doubt or envy. But a thought is not a sin until we entertain it. If we say "NO!" at once and turn to the Lord for help, we are not sinning. It is when we close our eyes and indulge ourselves in the thought that it separates us from God.'

After a few weeks Josie told me that Satan had soon become tired of his game of mental darts.

Our attitudes can separate us from God

In the first chapter of Isaiah (verses 15–17) God says, 'Even though you make many prayers, I will not hear . . . wash yourself . . . Learn to do good, to be fair and to help the poor, the fatherless and widows.' (LB) In other words, God will not hear us if we are bullying someone who is in our power. Is there a pupil in your class, or a child in your family who always seems to get the rough side of your tongue? An office junior, an elderly relation, even your own husband or wife! God wants us to build people up with encouragement, not browbeat them by constant nagging or criticism.

Many people do not dare to do their bullying face to face, they prefer to destroy people behind their backs by niggling comments. I have come to believe that critical, cynical remarks and a harsh, unloving attitude towards

---

If I had cherished sin in my heart the Lord would not have listened. Psalm 66:18

other people are one of the most common causes of spiritual deserts.

We all know lies are wrong

We all know lies are wrong, but 'white lies make people happy', we argue, 'half truths are kinder' and 'exaggeration makes a better story'. God must hate the smiling masks behind which we hide our real thoughts from other Christians.

Spiritual pride

In Woolworths one day I overheard Mrs P talking about Robbie, the girl mentioned on page 28.

'Fancy!' said this righteous pillar of the women's fellowship, 'I would never dream of going off with someone else's husband!' Perhaps she would not, but she was forgetting that pride is as bad in God's eyes as adultery.

Jesus told us about a really good man who went up to pray in the temple – but God did not hear a word he said because of his attitude towards someone else. The Pharisee *did* nothing to the sinner hiding in the corner, he did not spit contemptuously or stone the man, he simply despised him mentally. (Luke 18:9–14)

When you think of your Christian friends, do you look *up* at them with respect, or look *down* on them for being less spiritual than you are? 'She can't speak in tongues yet, poor thing.' Or 'How sad that they're all so shallow.'

But how can I ever know what sins are lurking in my heart? Cleanse me from these hidden faults. And keep me from deliberate wrongs. Psalm 19:12–13, LB

The harder we strive after a holy life, the more likely we are to fall into the unholy trap of spiritual pride. 'Be humble towards one another, always considering others better than yourselves' (Philippians 2:3). When we cannot seem to give God worship, we need to remember that the kind He loves most is the offering of a humble, repentant heart. (Psalm 51:17)

A rebellious streak

Some people are always slightly 'agin' the government of the day. They have to mock or criticise their vicar or church leaders and 'cut them down to size'. 'Obey your leaders and follow their orders,' says Hebrews chapter 13 verse 17. If you honestly feel you cannot follow and respect your church leaders then you are either separating yourself from God by a rebellious attitude, or you could be in the wrong church.

Broken relationships

'I just can't seem to get through to God any more,' complained Yvonne, 'my Christian life's gone dead on me.'

'Have you asked God why?' I said.

Next Sunday Yvonne was sitting in church when verses 23–24 from Matthew 5 were read as part of the second lesson. 'So if you are about to offer your gift to God at the altar and there you remember that your brother has something against you, leave your gift there

> *Our iniquities, our secret heart and its sins, (which we would so like to conceal even from ourselves;) You have set in the (revealing) light of your countenance.* Psalm 90:8, AMP

in front of the altar, go at once and make peace with your brother and then come back and offer your gift.'

Suddenly she realised that the beginning of her desert had coincided with a fierce row she had with Mrs P over the church flower rota. They had never liked each other and used the heat of battle to tell each other so – volubly.

'I *was* rather mean to the poor old biddy,' thought Yvonne as she realised just how much that argument had bothered her subconsciously.

'I felt like jumping up there and then and doing what the verse told me to do – putting matters right at once before I attempted to worship,' she told me later. 'But I managed to wait until Mrs P was pouring the after-service coffee before I told her I wanted to apologise.

'She slammed the kettle down and said, "About time too, young lady!" I was so upset. She just couldn't see that it was as much her fault as mine! But later in the day, I went for a long walk and realised I had done what Jesus told me to do, and it was not my fault if she didn't respond. I've felt close to Him ever since and I can worship again at last.'

If our relationships are wrong, and we owe someone an apology or need to forgive them for some damage they have done to us, we will feel separated from God until we do something about it.

Thou shalt worship the Lord thy God and Him only shalt thou serve

It is terribly hard to keep that first great commandment in these days when most people worship 'things'.

Conscious repentance leads to unconscious holiness. Roy Hession

'In our first little rented flat we were so happy together and with the Lord,' said Catherine wistfully. 'Then we began using all our time and energy buying the perfect home. The most important thing in Ray's life was to get as high as possible in his firm, and for me it was to have the same 'things' as the others in our circle – a microwave oven, a dishwasher, a BMW car with a telephone, a size ten body and a foreign sun tan. Soon these things had become our bosses, but we did not realise we were worshipping them instead of God. We always went to church, unless of course it clashed with a golf match.

Then, suddenly, Ray was made redundant, and we got into financial hot water. In fact we looked like losing everything; even our marriage was falling apart. It was then that we remembered that Jesus said, "You cannot serve both God and money." (Luke 16:13) If ony we had put Him in the centre of our lives the job and the "things" wouldn't have become so important.'

It is not a sin to be rich. The Bible says the love of money, not money itself, is the root of all evil, but as Christians we need to ask ourselves who owns our possessions – us or God?

Because we live in this sin-filled world, we tend to absorb the attitudes and behaviour of the people around us. But if we ask Him, God will insert a completely new disk into our mental computer and reprogram all our thoughts. 'Do not conform yourselves to the standards of

---

Jesus said: 'The seeds that fell among thorn bushes stand for those who hear; but the worries and riches and pleasures of this life crowd in and choke them, and their fruit never ripens.' Luke 8:14

this world, but let God transform you inwardly by a complete change of your mind. – Then you will be able to know . . . what is good and is pleasing to Him.' (Romans 12:2)

Addiction – the habit Satan says we cannot kick

'Mine iniquities have taken hold upon me, so that I am not able to look up . . .' (Psalm 40:12) That is exactly how we feel when we are gripped by a habit or addiction which keeps on trapping us in the desert.

'Satan's really got me by the throat this time,' we think miserably. But Satan is nothing but a beaten bully who likes us to remember verse 8 in 1 Peter 5, which says '. . . the Devil roams round like a roaring lion looking for someone to devour', while he prefers us to miss James Chapter 4 verse 7, which tells us that if we resist him he has to run away!

Fifteen years ago I was in a horrible desert and I felt utterly defeated by a habit I just could not kick. I knew it was wrong and God had told me clearly to remove it from my life. I would manage for several days and then give in to it yet again.

'Sorry Lord,' I would say and then I would get up from my knees and stagger on through the day, forgiven but feeling uncomfortable because I knew I was secretly looking forward to the next fall. My will wanted the enjoyment of the habit more than it wanted to obey God, and that troubled my conscience. Soon all I ever seemed

> . . . *obeying God with deep reverence, shrinking back from all that might displease Him. For God is at work within you, helping you want to obey Him and then helping you do what He wants.* Philippians 2:12–13

to say to God was 'sorry'. My comfortable relationship
with Him was ruined. It never occurred to me to ask God
to take possession of my will, as well as the rest of me.

Vital fact

A very few fortunate people are cured of their addiction
instantly to such things as nicotine, alcohol, drugs,
over-eating or sexual wrong-doing. They are free as a
result of just one prayer. Most of us struggle with our
particular weakness all our lives. Far from feeling 'let
down' by this, we need to revel in the fact that we grow
closer to God when we have to rely on Him daily and
even hourly for power to resist temptation. I did not
know that then, so I felt annoyed with God for not
making things easier for me.

One day, I went into a country churchyard to kill time
while I waited for the post office to open. In a corner I
discovered a life-sized crucifix and as I looked up into the
Lord's face, I was horrified by the suffering and stark
agony portrayed there. Perhaps it was a trick of the light,
or the brilliance of the artist – or was it a vision? Suddenly
the face was no longer a sculpture, it was real. I saw the
drops of sweat, the bruises and the blood that trickled
down from His crown of thorns. He had gone through all
this to break the chains that bound me, yet I had been
busy forging the links again with the sins and dis-

---

*So then, let us rid ourselves of everything that gets
in the way, and of the sin which holds on to us so
tightly, and let us run with determination the race
that lies before us.*

Let us keep our eyes fixed on Jesus. Hebrews
12:1–2

obediences I had been treating so casually. My attitude mocked His agony and suddenly something inside me broke as I stood there in helpless tears of true repentance.

We come out of the deserts we cause ourselves when we realise just how intensely our sins hurt Jesus and how much He minds the loss of our company.

My mind and my body may grow weak, but God is my strength; He is all I ever need. *Psalm 73:26*

2: THE DESERT ASSOCIATED WITH PHYSICAL ILLNESS AND FATIGUE

Nothing can smother spiritual verve more rapidly than a cold in the head! So often, when we feel flat spiritually, we torture ourselves by unnecessary guilt, when all the time our desert has a purely physical origin.

We are made up of three parts: body, soul and mind. When our bodies are functioning below par, our minds may become depressed and our souls can feel far from God. Many spiritual problems actually stem from:

* Hormone imbalance
* Overwork or 'ministry burn-out'
* Vitamin deficiencies
* The side effects of a prescribed drug
* Prolonged stress
* Illness for which we should be receiving medical help

Meet your body's needs first

When Jesus went into his desert, Satan waited until He was physically weak from fasting and dehydration, then he attacked. Satan knows that when the bodies of human beings are weak, their minds and souls are more vulnerable to him. Perhaps it is our bodies that need to be cosseted and prayed over before we begin to worry about our souls!

God knew that was Elijah's first need. He had just been through a huge time of stress on top of three years of scanty food when he ran away into the desert, lay down under a bush and wished to die. God allowed him first to sleep and then He sent an angel with some good food before He took the old Prophet away alone and gave him a fresh revelation of Himself. A holiday, with plenty of good food, fresh air and early nights, can often do wonders for the soul!

When we are at that initial stage of asking 'why Lord?' (see Chapter 2) it is often sensible to have a medical check up. One friend of mine felt her Christian life was disintegrating until she discovered she had a thyroid deficiency which her doctor easily remedied.

When we are ill, Christians have easy access to the best doctor in the world, Jesus Himself. Naturally, we turn to Him first – He may heal us miraculously, work through medical science or He may delay our healing completely for a time.

Often while we wait for healing we go into a desert

Sometimes we feel closer to God when we are acutely ill than at any other time in our lives. He positively hovers over that hospital bed. It is when we grind on month after month never feeling any better that God seems far away.

> *The menopause has a lot of deserts to answer for.*
> Elizabeth Church

Perhaps we are told the illness is going to be lengthy or even a permanent part of our lives. 'Why doesn't He answer my prayer?' we ask miserably.

When we can no longer dash round for God or be busily involved in all kinds of Church work, we feel strangely devalued in His sight. That is just how a friend of mine was feeling when her brother Alan said something to her which literally changed her life:

> 'It is not what we do for God that matters
> but what we will allow Him to do for us.'

'My power shows up best in weak people.' (2 Corinthians 12:9, LB)

So when our arms and legs feel like cotton wool, it is then and only then that we discover the full extent of God's power. Satan tells us we are useless, (self-confidence always goes when we are ill) but it always seems to slip Satan's mind that we are actually no good to God when we trust our own abilities. It is only when we have to rely on God completely that we become useful to Him. The moment we realise that, Satan is defeated.

> 'A weak person who has nothing to rely on but the strength of God is one hundred times more powerful spiritually than an ordinary strong human being,' said Annette, who has multiple sclerosis.

If God had wanted to breed a race of supermen to be His earthly children, He would not have chosen

When your liver is upset, your prayer life will suffer. David Pawson

'what the world considers weak in order to shame the powerful'. (1 Corinthians 1:27)

The healing epidemic

If I had become ill twenty years ago, I do not think I would have gone into a spiritual desert at all. It was only because I had been taught to expect healing on demand that I felt I had failed God and He had failed me. Since I wrote *Beyond Healing*, I have become increasingly concerned about the huge number of Christians who have gone into deserts because they have not recovered even when they had apparently fulfilled all the Bible's conditions for healing. I have received many letters like this one from Diane.

> I know God heals people, I've seen Him do it! I'm excited that the Church has rediscovered something that lay dormant for so long. When I became ill I was sure God was going to heal me, the whole Church prayed, fasted and the elders anointed me with oil, (James 5) but I still felt ill.
>
> 'Don't think about the symptoms,' they said, 'that's just Satan pretending', so I flushed my pills down the loo and told my doctor I wouldn't need them any more. I used every atom of my energy trying to convince myself and the world that I was well, I even told people lies.
>
> 'I'm fine,' I would say brightly. 'I'm perfectly fit now,

I am most happy then, to be proud of my weaknesses, in order to feel the protection of Christ's power over me . . . For when I am weak, then I am strong. 2 Corinthians 12:9–10

I've been healed.' But gradually it dawned on me that I was not. The pills I had flushed away were actually vital to my life. I was so embarrassed when the doctor was called out in the night, and I had to explain. I felt I had let the whole Church down, they said it was my fault and I didn't have enough faith or will power. I was so ashamed I left, but now I don't feel I fit into any Church somehow. I'm a complete failure.

How dare we do that kind of thing to our Christian brothers and sisters? Sometimes God has to allow a period of illness so we can discover certain of the more precious treasures of darkness. We are robbed of them when people cover us in condemnation.

I overheard a conversation at the supermarket check out the other day, 'Its only your health that matters', muttered one woman to her friend as they both looked at me in my wheelchair. A fly on the wall during some prayer meetings could be forgiven for feeling that Christians now agree with the world on the question of physical fitness. When we lay too much emphasis on the healing ministry, are we not denying the fact that the soul is permanent while the body is very temporary? Even Mr Universe and Miss World will be old age pensioners in a few years' time!

So, if you do happen to be ill, stop feeling guilty. Stop using so much energy agitating to be well that you have none left to dig for the gemstones down in those mines. The treasure God may want you to discover is that He still

> *For this reason we never become discouraged. Even though our physical being is gradually decaying, yet our spiritual being is renewed day after day.* 2 Corinthians 4:16

can heal miraculously. So go on believing in miracles, but keep digging in the meantime!

Not 'one day at a time' – a day can feel like an eternity!

Even though God may not restore all our strength to us in one go, He never leaves us without enough for the things we really *have* to do. In his letter to the Philippians Chapter 4 verse 13 St Paul says, 'For I can do everything God asks me to with the help of Christ who gives me the strength and power.'

Recently I heard from my friend Clem who has been ill for many years. He has learnt to break his days up into short sections.

God prepares parcels of strength and leaves them hidden behind every milestone along the way ahead. As we run out of strength during the day, we pray, and then pick up the next parcel.

How that helped me. Sometimes I will be sitting in my chair and I think, 'I just haven't the energy to get the supper tonight'. I have to bend down in prayer and pick up another parcel of strength which will carry me on to the next milestone.

> When we have exhausted our store of
>   endurance,
> When our strength has failed ere the day is half
>   done.
> When we reach the end of our hoarded
>   resources,
> Our Father's full giving is only begun.
> Annie Johnson Flint

'O God my Rock,' I cry, 'why have You forsaken me? Why must I suffer . . . O my soul, don't be discouraged. Don't be upset. Expect God to act! For I know that I shall again have plenty of reason to praise Him for that that He will do. *Psalm 42:9–11, LB*

3: THE DESERT OF DEPRESSION

'I wouldn't describe my depression as a desert,' said Janet, 'to me it felt more like a dark pit in the desert!'

'WHY do Christians always spiritualise depression?' demanded another friend, Pat. 'If I'd been in a general hospital half the Church would have visited me, loaded with grapes and chocolates, but because I was in the psychiatric wing, they only came near me to say I must be harbouring some unconfessed sin, or unresolved conflict. Someone even said, "self-pity is at the bottom of all depressions". It's funny how people who aren't depressed always know just what depressed people ought to do!'

There is nothing a human being can go through which is worse than severe depression. The Bible says, 'A man's spirit sustains him in sickness, but a crushed spirit who can bear?' (Proverbs 18:14, NIV) When you go through physical pain, grief or adversity, you can turn to God for support, but often one of the symptoms of depression is that you feel you have lost Him as well.

Depression is not a sin, or a sign of failure
Depression is a normal part of human life from which

Christians are not exempt. Some of the greatest people of God down the centuries have suffered from bouts of depression. Jeremiah, David, Elijah, John Wesley and Lord Shaftesbury. Spurgeon was sometimes too depressed to climb into his pulpit on a Sunday, while Martin Luther, 'sobbed himself into his last sleep like a great wearied child'. William Cowper is alleged to have attempted suicide the day he wrote 'God moves in a mysterious way his wonders to perform,' and perhaps the greatest charismatic of our day, David Watson, also admitted he was frequently depressed. So perhaps it is time we all stopped feeling so embarrassed about an illness which is no more shameworthy than breaking a leg.

My trouble was I thought my problem was spiritual when in fact I was simply suffering from post viral depression. I battled away alone, too ashamed to admit how terrible I felt, even to my family. I thought if I went to my doctor he would label me as a 'nut case', and if I went to my minister he would think of me as a failure.

There are reasons why so many of us confuse physical illness with the 'dark night of the soul'.

Symptoms of depression
The normal symptoms of depression make us feel:

* God no longer loves, forgives or accepts us.
* He no longer even exists.

> O my soul, why be so gloomy and discouraged? Trust in God! He will make me smile again for He is my God! Psalm 43:5, LB

Acute anxiety

Anxiety often goes with depression and causes:

* Guilt about real or imaginary past sins.
* Fear of the future which robs us of our trust in God.
* Lack of concentration so we cannot read the Bible or pray.
* Fear of people which makes church impossible.

'Christians are the most difficult group of patients to treat,' explained the Christian doctor whom I consulted before writing this chapter. 'They find it so hard to admit they are depressed, particularly when the depression is not acute but long term or chronic. They, and their family, simply feel they have developed a naturally 'gloomy' personality. They may therefore function below their potential for years, feeling that their whole lives are grey and flat. They are always tired, lacking in enthusiasm and are unwilling to put much effort into life. Medical science could do so much to help them, if only they could be brave enough to go to their doctor, and receive his treatment as a gift from God.'

God really can heal the dark places in our lives and I am convinced that depressed Christians are closer to God's heart than any of His other children. I began to recover when I swallowed my pride and went to ask someone to pray for me. The healing took many months, but I know that day was the turn of the tide. Had I also gone to my doctor, his treatment could have been used by God as a supplement to prayer.

> *How long must I wrestle with my thoughts . . . ?*
> *How long will my enemy triumph over me . . . ?*
> *Answer me, O Lord my God; give light to my eyes*
> *or I will sleep in death.* Psalm 13:2–3

The Lord dwells in clouds and darkness
(2 Chronicles 6:1)

Whether we tackle our 'grey fog' with the ministry of healing, through modern medicine or through both, we will probably find our depression lifts much more slowly than we would like. How can we cope while we wait?

When Jane rang me she was right at the 'bottom of the pit'.

'I can't think why I'm 'phoning you,' she began, 'there is absolutely nothing you can say that won't irritate me. I love the Lord so much, yet He stands by and allows me to feel like this. Don't say anything,' she added hurriedly, 'there's no answer to that one either!'

'Surely there must be something that helps?' I said trying not to sound glib.

'John 1:5,' she snapped. 'That's what keeps me alive. "The light shines in the darkness and the darkness has never put it out." Often I feel in such darkness it almost chokes me, but I always know, deep down that the light *is* there, even if I can't see it and the darkness *has* never, *can* never and *will* never extinguish it.' Perhaps Jane was expressing her 'treasure of darkness' when she added, 'When you hurt so much that you feel you couldn't possibly hurt any more, your need for God is paramount. When you reach that stage you really know Him.'

Pooh Bear was Janet's 'treasure of darkness'

'Just praise the Lord, dear,' someone said to Janet as she struggled with weeks of post-operative depression. She

---

The Lord is close to the broken hearted, and saves those who are crushed in spirit. Psalm 34:18

reacted just like most depressed people when given such advice – she felt wild! It may be a biblical command, but it is one we all find practically impossible when we are acutely depressed.

'I really did try,' admitted Janet, 'but somehow I didn't feel He loved me any more. I always felt ghastly when I first woke in the morning and I remember once I sat up racking my brains, trying to think of something I could thank the Lord for, when I seemed to have lost all purpose in life.

'I heard the children down in the kitchen, could I thank Him for them? No! I wanted to be a bright cheerful Mum again, but I was letting them down by my gloom.

'Neil perhaps? No, I was being a rotten wife.

'My friends? No, I ought to ring them all and thank them for the cakes they had left on the doorstep, but I couldn't work up the courage.

'My bedroom then? No it was dusty and untidy. I ought to clean it, but I had no energy. I couldn't even decide what to put on that day. Surely there was something, just one small thing in all the world worthy of a 'thank you?'

'Then my attention was caught by the toy Pooh Bear we had bought for our niece's birthday. He just sat there on the dressing table, holding out his arms to be loved. He had no purpose in life either! He was useless really, but I couldn't help loving him.

"If I can love Pooh," I thought, "just because he sits

Ye may yourself ebb and flow, rise and fall, wax and wane, but your Lord is this day as He was yesterday. Samuel Rutherford there holding out his arms to me, then surely God can love me, when I do the same to Him." Suddenly I found I could thank God for Pooh, as I hugged his furry body.

'It no longer mattered that I couldn't pray, God knew how I needed Him, even though I was as incapable as Pooh Bear of telling Him so.

'Somehow we never managed to give that Pooh away, because he was the beginning of my recovery. We had to buy another for my niece's birthday.'

There are no easy answers to depression. The one and only thing that helped me was the realisation that Jesus knows from bitter, personal experience just what it feels like. He cried out in His darkness,

'My God, My God, why have you abandoned me.' He told His Father just how ghastly He was feeling, and when I dared to do the same, I began to recover.

(As for me), I am poor and needy, yet the Lord takes thought and plans for me. *Psalm 40:17*

4: THE DESERT OF FAILURE AND WORTHLESSNESS

One of the earliest replies to my 'desert enquiries' came from a vicar's wife in London.

Thy love to me, Oh God, not mine, Oh Lord to Thee, can rid me of this dark unrest and set my spirit free. Horatius Bonar

For years I have struggled with a crushing sense of worthlessness, of not feeling adequate. I always seem to make a mess of things, and feel sure God must think the same.

'How strange,' I thought, 'outwardly she always seems so successful, running the parish and a rambling old vicarage just like clockwork. While all the time, she secretly feels a failure.'

I used to think I was the only one who felt inadequate, but I am beginning to realise lots of us suffer from low self-esteem. Most of the time we manage to disguise it by flurries of Christian activity, but when something goes seriously wrong in our lives, the buried sense of inferiority bobs up to the surface again. We think, 'It's no wonder my husband left me – I lost my job – didn't get healed – I always was unlovable and unsuccessful.' Because we feel sure God must share the low opinion we have of ourselves, we go into a desert.

We live in a success-orientated world, and even as Christians we measure ourselves and one another by our achievements. We set ourselves impossibly high goals and feel useless to both God and man when we cannot attain them. When will we learn that God does not look at what we do, He looks at what we are?

I remember, years ago, standing at a sink full of greasy washing up and thinking, 'I'm nothing but a mess!' I had always dreamed of doing some great thing for God – being a missionary perhaps or an evangelist, but all I had become was an ordinary and very unsuccessful housewife. My cakes were always soggy, my children drove me

Be patient with everyone, but above all with yourself. Francis de Sales

up the walls and I couldn't even knit! I was fat, tired and defeated.

'Get out and meet other Christians,' someone had urged me. That made me feel worse. They all seemed to be so successful, praying out loud so beautifully, leading people to the Lord over the garden fence and having wonderful experiences, revelations and spiritual gifts. Nothing I tried to do for God ever worked.

Have you ever felt like that? I was certainly in a desert of worthlessness, and I escaped it by a chance encounter with a complete stranger.

One afternoon my mother-in-law had the kids to tea and I went into Tunbridge Wells in gorgeous solitude. I was browsing round the Christian bookshop, trying not to break my latest diet by visiting the cake shop near by, when I heard someone say,

'Ah! How perfectly lovely!' I had not noticed the elderly man standing beside me, we were both too absorbed in the books, so I jumped violently.

He was holding the newly published *Good News Bible* and suddenly he thrust it towards me, open at the book of Zephaniah. His gnarled finger was jabbing excitedly towards verse 17 of Chapter 3.

'The Lord your God is with you . . . The Lord will take delight in you and in His love He will give you new life. He will sing and be joyful over you.'

'What more do we want in life but to know that!' he exclaimed, and then, suddenly looking terribly British and embarrassed, he lifted his hat nervously, and scut-

---

Jesus said, 'He has sent me to . . . deliver those who are oppressed . . . downtrodden, bruised, crushed and broken down by calamity.' Luke 4:18, AMP

tled out of the shop. He probably felt a complete fool for the rest of the day, but when I arrive in heaven I shall tell him that his enthusiastic explosion caused scales to fall from my eyes. I stood gazing after him, positively quivering with joy.

'All right, so I'm a fat, spotty nobody, but God who made the whole universe takes delight *in me!* He even sings about me!' Other customers jostled round me, but still I stood there, as if bathed in God. Inside my head a voice said, 'You are the centre of the universe for Me. Nothing is more important to Me than your welfare. He who touches you, touches the apple of My eye. If you had been the only sinner in the world, I would still have been willing to be tortured, disgraced and killed, just so I could win you for myself.'

In those days I could still dance, and I have often wondered what people thought when they saw me waltz out of the shop! Whenever those old worthless feelings threaten me, as they still often do, I think of that day with joy and relief.

Many deserts are caused by looking at other people

As a small girl I was once 'dared' to walk along the high wall that separated the senior and junior playgrounds – I did not dare at all, but even in those days my desire to be

---

God loves each one of us as if there was only one of us to love. St Augustine

---

Oh Lord, You protect me and save me, Your care has made me great. Psalm 18:35

accepted by the group overpowered my common sense.
As they hoisted me up someone whispered, 'Keep looking at the white gatepost.' I had no idea what she meant
until I was up on the wall and the world was spinning
round me. If I looked down at all the other children
jumping about and shouting their encouragement on
either side of me I would certainly topple to disaster. If I
looked at my own feet I was also doomed, but ahead of
me at the far end of my ordeal was the white ball on top of
the stone gatepost. Keeping my eyes fixed on that and
walking steadily towards it saved my neck.

Sadly, my hour of glory was short-lived. The head-
mistress had been looking out of her window. Yet I can
never read verse 2 in Hebrews Chapter 12, without
thinking of that day.

'Let us keep our eyes fixed on Jesus, on whom our faith
depends from beginning to end.' It is what God thinks of
us that counts, not how we feel about ourselves, or how
we compare with other Christians.

The modern cult of 'love yourself'

Almost every Christian book you open these days seems
to tell you to love yourself and shows you how to build up
your self-esteem. For lots of us that is quite impossible.
We really do dislike ourselves because we feel we are
rather inadequate people. Trying to build your own
self-esteem feels like lifting a bucket you happen to be
standing in! The only way out of this self-hating desert is

*Instruments that the world would have flung on
the scrap heap with infinite contempt, have again
and again in the hand of the Master worked
wonders.* W. S. Watkinson

to look straight into God's face. It is not our *self*-esteem we should be building, but our *God*-esteem.

If you feel crushed because you have never been any good at anything, stop worrying about it! You are just the kind of person God wants. Jesus said it would be the meek and humble who would inherit the earth! He finds it harder to use people with many natural talents and glittering personalities. They tend to take His glory for themselves. He wants to show how powerful He is by using people who rely on Him utterly because they have nothing to be proud of in themselves.

Like a child on a high wall, we need to stop looking down at our inferiority complexes, or sideways at our successful friends and start concentrating all our attention on Jesus, revelling in what He can do for us and not in what we can do for Him. He says to everyone who feels worthless; 'I am the high and holy God, who lives for ever. I live in a high and holy place . . . with people who are humble and repentant, so that I can restore their confidence and hope.' (Isaiah 57:15)

God says; 'The mountains and hills may crumble, but My love for you will never end; I will keep for ever My promise of peace.' Isaiah 54:10

So in my emptiness, waiting until,
I give my nothingness to be fulfilled,
Here, where no hand can touch, deep in my
  soul,
pours out His love divine, and makes me whole.
Estelle White

5: THE DESERT OF DELAYED SHOCK

Everyone was shattered when Phil's husband left her
and their three young children. It seemed unbelievable
that their marriage could break up, when they had both
been so involved in Christian activities. The whole
church gathered round Phil protectively, and her radiant
peace was a blessing to them all.

'That girl's a shining witness to the whole town,' said
one of the elders. Then, suddenly, a few months later
everything changed. Phil went into a desert.

'I think I was simply numb at first,' she told me, 'My
mind wasn't working, I kept looking down on myself
from above and thinking, "How wonderfully God is
helping her to cope." But I didn't really feel it was *me*. I
just floated along on the current of everyday events, I
didn't try and swim. I suppose I was sure David would
come back at any minute.

'Then one Saturday, I was out with the kids in the park.
All round us were families. Families with Dads, and the
shock finally hit me. It felt like being kicked in the
tummy. David had gone. He was living with Sue. My
kids would have to grow up without a Dad.

'Since then I seem to have lost my peace completely. I
know I need help, but people have drifted back to their
own lives, thinking I'm managing so well, but I'm falling
apart inside.

'The memory of some cruel thing David did or said hits
me unexpectedly when I'm right in the middle of doing

---

*He heals the broken-hearted and bandages up
their wounds.* Psalm 147:3
What wound did heal but by degrees. William
Shakespeare

something quite different, like peeling potatoes. Or perhaps I'll think, "it must have been all my fault. I ought to have lost some weight, been more appreciative, cooked better". Wherever I go, whatever I do, these thoughts keep on coming at me, like a swarm of bees buzzing in my head night and day. I can't pray because of them, or settle to read the Bible because these bitter thoughts make me feel so guilty. Why should all this happen to me *now*?'

I minded for Phil desperately, but I felt quite out of my depth so I suggested we prayed about it.

'You pray,' she said miserably, 'I'll listen.' As we sat there together before God, something wonderful happened. Phil saw a picture in her mind of a deep, sombre lake, and one by one up to the surface floated sodden logs of wood.

'I think this is a sign that you are getting better,' I said when she told me about it.

'*Better!*' she almost shouted, 'I've never felt worse in my life!'

'Look,' I said awkwardly. 'All the things you've been feeling are perfectly natural human reactions. When ghastly things happen to us, at first God protects our sanity by this numb feeling – rather as a doctor protects a gaping wound with a dressing. But you can't keep a dressing on a wound for ever. God has to remove it some time and allow all these reactions to come to the surface so He can heal them. He knows it would be too much for us to face them at the beginning, while we are still reeling from the initial blow.'

'I'd rather they'd stayed buried,' Phil complained.

God is nearer to us than we are to ourselves.
St Augustine

'But God wants you whole,' I replied, 'and He can't heal things until we admit they exist, and give them to Him.'

Two weeks later I rang Phil. She was still coping with what she called her 'Loch Ness monsters' as they broke the surface of her 'lake', one by one.

'Thoughts are so difficult to manage,' she said, 'They're so abstract. But when I suddenly think . . . "David took the cassette player and I paid for that!" I write down the way I feel on a piece of paper. Sometimes I have quite a struggle, I almost want to hug the hurt to myself. There's a crooked kind of enjoyment in feeling sorry for yourself. When I feel able to relinquish the pain to God, I go out into the kitchen, set light to the paper and flush the ashes down the sink. It is such a cleansing feeling.'

Phil's desert is quite a common one. As Christians we often get through horrific experiences on the crest of a spiritual wave, or 'floating on a lilo of other people's prayers'. We nurse our child through a terminal illness or keep our heads during a major crisis, but when the pressure is suddenly off, and no one is looking on any more, bang! We are hit by the devastating effects of delayed shock.

Confusing shock with deserts
Don't confuse the natural symptoms of shock with a desert. We have already seen that doubt was a natural

> *It is one thing to go through a crisis grandly, but another thing to go through every day, glorifying God when there is no witness, no limelight, no one paying the remotest attention to us.* Oswald Chambers

reaction for Ann when she lost her baby in a cot death. (Page 59) Other painful feelings are also part of the grieving process, such as anger, depression, guilt or loss of reality and even of God Himself. As Christians we feel so guilty about having these feelings, we are ashamed to look God in the face, but they are simply normal stages of human grief. Far from cutting us off from God, they can bring us even nearer to Him because: 'Surely He (Jesus) has borne our griefs – sickness, weakness and distress – and carried our sorrows and pain.' (Isaiah 53:4, AMP) No one can help us when we are laden with parcels and bulging shopping bags, unless we are willing to let them. Jesus longs to carry our griefs and sorrows, but we do have to hand them over to Him as the numbing effect of shock wears off and they come up to the surface one by one.

Answer me now, Lord! I have lost all hope. Don't hide Yourself from me, . . . Remind me each morning of Your constant love, for I put my trust in You. *Psalm 143:7–8*

6: THE DESERT OF UNANSWERED PRAYER

'I prayed night and morning for five years,' wrote Debbie, 'but God just didn't answer. What did I do wrong?'

God can do wonders with a broken heart if you give Him all the pieces. Victor Alfsen

For a Christian the problem of unanswered prayer can be sheer agony. As we beat on the prison walls of our circumstances we know without doubt that God could change them, but Heaven seems hard-bolted against our prayers.

'What did I do wrong?' asked Debbie, and of course the Bible clearly shows us that if we hold on to sin deliberately (Psalm 66:17–18) or persist in disobeying some specific instruction, the Lord cannot hear us. He says, 'Because they did not listen when I spoke, I did not answer when they prayed.' (Zechariah 7:13)

Yet, even after Debbie had given her life a thorough spring-clean, the answer to her prayer was still 'No'. Why? Seven 'principles of unanswered prayer' will help us to see a meaning behind the disappointments.

First principle – 'no' is not a punishment

* David said to God, 'Answer me quickly, O Lord, my spirit fails. Do not hide your face from me.' (Psalm 143:7)

* Job said, 'Why won't God give me what I ask, why won't He answer my prayer?' (Job 6:8)

* Paul said, 'Three times I prayed to the Lord about this, and asked Him to take it away. But His answer was: "My grace is all you need."' (2 Corinthians, 12:8–9)

These men lived as close to God as anyone ever has, and yet they still did not have their prayers answered.

Delayed answers to prayer are not only trials of faith but they give us opportunities to honour God by our steadfast confidence in Him under apparent repulses. C. H. Spurgeon

Even the man Jesus described as 'the greatest man who was ever lived'. His own cousin, John the Baptist, received a definite 'No' to his prayers.

When Herod's dungeon door slammed, John probably did not worry at first. He knew Jesus was the Messiah. Hadn't he seen the spirit of God descending on him by the river Jordan?

He knew Isaiah had foretold that the Messiah would not only make the blind see and the lame walk, but He would also set the captives free (Isaiah 61). 'I'll be out of here in no time!' John must have thought.

Then the weeks and months began to grind slowly by and John's prayers for freedom were not answered. It was torture being shut up in four walls after a lifetime in the wide expanse of the wilderness. Surely Jesus would come for him soon?

Delayed hope is the hardest test of faith. John began to doubt when God's promise appeared to be delaying.

'Are You the one we are waiting for, or should we be looking for some other man?' was the message he finally sent to Jesus.

Gently the Lord reminded him of Isaiah's prophecies which were being fulfilled as the lame walked and the blind received sight; yet for some reason He left out the one vital phrase about the release of captives, the only miracle that mattered to John in his prison.

Why? Jesus could so easily have burst that prison wide

When our hearts are turned to fear, rather than to faith we must hand over to God the mysteries of life's imbalance between good and evil. I find that if I mull too long over the things I don't understand I lose the things I do understand. Jean Darnall

open. He sent an angel and an earthquake to rescue his friends Peter and Paul. Why leave his own cousin to face a sordid death at the whim of a dancing girl and her vindictive mother?

Second principle – we might have wrong expectations of Jesus

John knew Gabriel had spoken to his father before he was born, and said that his life's work was to help the Messiah establish His earthly Kingdom. He thought that meant Jesus would give him the status of Prime Minister. Actually Jesus wanted to give him something far more important, the everlasting throne of a martyr. (Revelation 20:4)

Deserts often occur because we assume we know the will of God. We feel 'let down' because we want something so very much that we confuse our will with God's will.

Debbie was convinced God wanted her to marry Robin, because she loved him so much. He was always friendly when they met at church and occasionally he asked her out, but to him Debbie was just one of a whole crowd of single girls in their thirties. Yet she would happily have died for Robin. Desperately she clung to several promises she felt God had given her and prayed earnestly that Robin's feelings would become as deep as her own. There was nothing wrong with her faith, she went on confidently believing God would answer her

> *Thousands follow Christ when He gives them what they want, few follow Him when He confronts them with what He wants.* Selwyn Hughes

prayers right up to the day he married her best friend –
then she went into her desert.

'I am trusting the Lord for healing – trusting Him for
that job – for that house,' we say firmly, but are we
trusting Him for *anything*? Even if that 'anything' is not
our will, ambition or desire?

'Lord,' we so often pray, 'I'll do whatever you ask, but
I just cannot stay – childless – single – ill or poor. You *must*
answer this one prayer.'

The love that Jesus has for you and for me is so absolute
that He allowed no earthly desire of His own to stand
between us, not even his own life. He longs for us to
return His love with the same single-minded quality. Yet
so often, there is something we want more than we want
Him. Prayer can be our way of manipulating Him to gain
our own desire. All the time we are nagging Him, He
does know what is the very best for us, and how much He
must long for us to realise that fact.

Third principle – God never promised to make this life easy

'I thought,' continued Debbie's letter, 'God would be
on my side if I kept close to Him and did my best. I
thought He'd make everything easy and reward me
with a happy, trouble-free life.'

Yes, God has promised us an eternity of happiness,
health and prosperity, but for a brief time down here He
tells us things may be tough. Jesus told us the truly happy

---

*For this world is not our home, we are look-
ing forward to our everlasting home in Heaven.*
Hebrews, 13:14, LB

people are the poor, the hungry, the down-trodden, the
grieving, the hated 'because a great reward is kept for
you in heaven.' (Luke 6:20–23) He also promised, 'In this
world you *will* have trouble.' (John 16:33)

No one knows why Jesus did not rescue His cousin
from prison, but one thing is certain, it makes no difference whatsoever to John now! The fact that he spent a
few uncomfortable months in jail down here will be as
unimportant to him now as the blink of an eye. I remember once feeling furious with Paul as I read; 'This small
and temporary trouble we suffer will bring us a
tremendous and eternal glory, much greater than the
trouble'. (2 Corinthians 4:17)

'Small! Temporary! My foot!' I fumed. 'Paul's troubles
may have seemed like that, but he ought to try mine!'
When I descended from the ceiling I managed to read on;
'For we fix our attention, not on things that are seen, but
on things that are unseen. What can be seen lasts only for
a time, but what cannot be seen lasts for ever.' (2 Corinthians 4:18) I realised I had been feeling trapped and
crushed by my circumstances, because I was looking
at them with human eyes. When I imagined myself
standing, millions of years into eternity, I could look back
at myself stuck in a wheelchair and think, 'why ever was
she making such a fuss?'

What is God to us? Of course God could make us all
healthy and wealthy in this life, but if He did, people
would follow Him simply for what they could get out of
Him – right now.

> *Many people want to direct God, instead of re-
> signing themselves to be directed by Him, to
> show Him a way instead of passively following
> where He leads.* Madam Guyon.

When we are facing unanswered prayer we have to ask ourselves; 'Do I see God as an adjunct to my life, a lucky charm to grant my every wish, or do I see myself as an adjunct to Him as I kneel before Him and say "Master, what do you want me to do for you?"'

Fifth principle – God always answers prayer

It was a bottle of fruit juice that helped my friend Fran to understand that 'wait' is just as valid an answer as 'yes'.

She had been grappling with an unanswered prayer for over a year, so I was surprised when she came to see me one day smiling broadly.

'Yesterday evening I was in the kitchen when Joy demanded a drink,' she began, (Joy is thirteen months old).

'Ju! Ju! Ju!' she squealed. Immediately I began the routine that getting her a drink entails. Boiled the kettle, then cooled the water, fetched bottle and teat from the steriliser, found the juice, measured a spoonful, collected a clean bib – it all takes so long and Joy was getting frantic, holding on to my ankles and hampering my efforts to help her. She was far too young to understand that at her age she has to have boiled water, and it would scald her if she drank it right from the kettle. I was doing all I could, as quickly as I could, but in her baby mind I was simply not caring about her thirst. I suddenly realised that quite probably God has the answer to my problems in the pipeline, but my human mind is too infantile to understand heavenly

What matter in eternity the slight awkwardness of time? Robert Murray M'Cheyne

procedures. I've been like Joy, holding on to His ankles and slowing Him down.'

Fran found the answer 'wait' a lot easier to cope with than the resounding 'No', which Debbie received.

Sixth principle – 'No' can be the best answer

Jesus once prayed, 'Father, save Me from this hour.' But the answer He received was, 'No'. His Father could have stopped the crucifixion, but He did not, because He knew that it would save mankind and glorify Jesus for ever. There are times when God's love for us will allow us also to suffer, and not answer our prayers by removing the pain. Paul, who three times received the answer 'No' to his most earnest prayer was able to say, '*In* all these things we have complete victory through Him that loved us.' (Romans 8:37) *In* them, not *by* having them removed.

I don't know why your child died, why you never had the baby you wanted so much, why you go to bed lonely every night of your life, why God has not healed me yet. No human being is wise enough to answer the question 'why doesn't God prevent suffering when He has the power?' In our pain and confusion we just have to reach out and say 'Father I do not understand you but I trust you.'

One of the hardest things in our secret prayer life is to accept with joy and not with grief the answers to our deepest prayers. It was a long time before I discovered that whatever came was the answer. I had expected something so different that I did not recognise it when it came. And He doesn't explain, He trusts us not to be offended, that's all.
Amy Carmichael

Seventh principle – God always gives us strength

'In the day when I cried, thou answeredst me, and strengthenedst me with strength in my soul,' says Psalm 138 verse 3. AV. God always answers our prayer *the split second* that we cry to Him; when the answer has to be 'wait' or even 'No', He always gives us strength, deep inside to carry us through, if only we will turn to Him for it.

Ridley said to Latimer as they were about to be burnt at the stake, 'Be of good cheer brother, for God will either assuage the fury of the flames, or else strengthen us to abide it,' God always does one or the other. He never leaves us alone in the fire.

I know how hard you have worked . . . but . . . you do not love Me now as you did at first. *Revelation 2:2–4*

7: THE DESERT OF PRESSURE AND OVERWORK

'I've got three kids under four. I love them, but a mountain of dirty nappies seems to be separating me

> *Dear brothers, you are only visitors here. Since your real home is in Heaven . . .* 1 Peter 2:11, LB
>
> *If contentment were here, Heaven were not Heaven.* Samuel Rutherford

from God; and coping with a hundred and one jobs all at once is making me too tired to do anything about it.'

There do seem to be definite periods in our lives when the sheer weight of unavoidable activities crowds out the things of God for a while. Working for exams, rebuilding, redecorating or moving house, starting a business, embarking on a new career or nursing elderly or dying relatives. In fact, I had more letters from people talking about the deserts caused by small children than any other, and I am not surprised either, having had six of my own!

Satan likes to use these 'pressure patches' to separate us from God, but I believe there are four ways we can prevent him from doing so, if we remember that:

Under such pressure we may forget God
We may feel we have lost God behind a 'mountain' of hard work, revision – or even dirty nappies, but He wants us to know that He is with us on our side of the mountain.

It does not matter if, for a while, we have to curtail our church activities. God is not only to be found in the Wednesday prayer meeting, He is standing beside us continuously as we work.

In 1660, there lived a monk called Brother Lawrence. He became deeply upset when his work in the monastery kitchen crowded thoughts of God from his mind, so he developed this coping strategy which has blessed busy

---

He will keep in perfect peace all those who trust in Him, whose thoughts turn often to the Lord.
Isaiah 26:3

Christians ever since. He visualised God there with him in the hectic kitchen continuously, both watching him and enjoying his company. Soon 'I could not pick up so much as a straw from the ground without doing it for Him. The time of business does not, with me, differ from the times of prayer, and in the noise and clatter of my kitchen, while several persons are at the same time calling for different things, I possess God in as great a tranquillity as if I were upon my knees at the blessed sacrament.'

A few moments each day for God

'Our duty to God,' said William Temple during an address at Oxford, 'requires that we should, for a good part of our time, be not consciously thinking about Him. That makes it absolutely necessary (if our life is to be a life of fellowship with Him,) that we shall have our times which are worship – pure and simple.'

That is easier said than done when you are a mother, working a twenty-six-hour day! But here are a few tips that might help.

'I always kept my *Daily Light* on the edge of the bath. Over twelve years I got through several copies, I kept dropping them in!'   (Ginny)

'All I wanted was to be alone with God, but Mums never *are* alone. So I kept a Bible in the loo. It may sound irreverent, but I used to read another verse

For the eyes of the Lord range throughout the earth to strengthen those whose hearts are fully committed to Him. 2 Chronicles 16:9 NIV

every time I went in there and it became a real place of sanctuary for me over the years.'   (Madeleine)

Mrs Billy Graham, the mother of five, and a housewife with a constantly open home, describes how she took her Bible round the house with her from room to room, and dug into it as she stirred a sauce or waited for the kettle to boil.

My own grandmother had seven children, and they can all remember her, kneeling beside the sofa, deep in prayer while they all played around her and two small boys bounced on her back.

In these days of cassettes in cars and kitchen, and even personal stereos in rush hour trains, we can all listen to the greatest preachers in the world, or the finest actors reading the scriptures. Many postal tape libraries are even free of charge.

Our attitude is the key

'I always wanted children,' Madeleine told me, 'but when they arrived I was astounded by my reaction. I resented them. They interfered with what I thought of as "my ministry", playing the church organ and training a large choir. My husband was the vicar so he was always out serving the Lord, while I felt trapped behind cot bars – useless to God. Then one day I visited another clergy wife and over her kitchen sink I saw this notice:

Think not of a holy life, for that will crush you by its immensity, think rather of this moment, and spend it for God. A holy life is but a series of holy moments. Lindsey Glegg

HERE I AM, SERVING GOD,
JUST WHERE GOD WANTS ME TO BE,
DOING WHAT GOD WANTS ME TO DO,
UNTIL GOD TELLS ME TO DO SOMETHING ELSE.

That had a profound effect on me. I realised I was out of touch with the Lord, because I wanted to serve Him in a more exciting way than just looking after kids. St Paul, stuck in prison, wrote, "I have learned the secret of being content in any and every situation . . . I can do everything through Him who gives me strength. (Phil. 4:12–13 NIV) God wanted me to learn that secret too.

One night something happened which I suppose you would call my treasure of darkness. I was reading Matthew 25 verse 40, in bed. "Whenever you did this for one of the least important of these brothers of mine, you did it for me." As usual I was up and down all night long to the children, till I was almost at screaming point. Then as I was giving yet another drink to Timmy, I remembered the verse I had read, and realised that it was *Jesus* Himself who was thirsty – Jesus in Timmy. I did not need to run meetings or train choirs to serve Him, I could simply love Him as I cared for the children.' (Mark 9:37)

We need to get back to God

'Suddenly my dear old mother-in-law was safe in Heaven, and I had time again. *Time – beautiful time!'*

Nothing done for Christ is lost. The smallest acts, the quietest words, the gentlest inspirations that touch human souls leave their impress for eternity. J. R. Miller

said Jean. 'Should I take up pottery, join the golf club or do a part-time job and earn some pin money? How easy it would have been to fill the vacuum with pleasant little interests, all perfectly all right in themselves, but I remembered in time that when I had been young, and without responsibilities, how much I had enjoyed spending my life doing things for God. I have watched too many of my friends drift into a middle-aged desert caused by ease and prosperity.

There's an old Arabian proverb which says, "All sunshine makes a desert."

I am so busy now in God's service I hardly have time to breathe, but I simply could not be happier!'

May we be refreshed as by streams in the desert.
Psalm 126:4

Is my gloom, after all,
Shade of His hand, outstretched caressingly?
Francis Thompson; from *The Hound of Heaven*

We do not know what to do, but we look to You for
help. *2 Chron. 20:12*

8: THE DESERT OF ACUTE ANXIETY
AND CHRONIC WORRY

Much has been written about worry, and most of it is
thoroughly irritating! 'If you worry you don't trust, if you
trust you don't worry.' That is the cliché placid, easy-
going people love to quote, but if a stressful situation is
causing you acute anxiety or you happen to be the
nervous kind, worry becomes something you cannot
remove, however much you try.

Once I was sitting on a tree stump in a wood reading an
Agatha Christie novel, when I chanced to look up and see
a rabbit only a few metres away from me. It was motion-
less, frozen by terror, as it looked at the swaying body of a
weasel which was about to spring at its throat. The rabbit
could run much faster than the weasel, but it was no
good preaching that fact to the rabbit, who was totally
paralysed by fear.

Worry can do the same thing to human beings, making
our minds go into a state of spasm.

'I've got to have a major operation . . . sit an exam . . .
start a new job . . . could this be cancer? . . . what if I die?'
As paralysed as that rabbit, we feel unable to move
towards God for His help.

Vital fact
We don't actually have to move towards Him, because
He is with us, on our side of the worries.

When I was about ten I went on the Sunday School
outing to Hastings. While our teacher slept on the beach,

we crept off to sample the forbidden delights of the pier. The ghost-train fascinated us.

'I dare you go on that all by yourself,' they said and like the 'sucker' that I always was, I swallowed the bait. Never in my life can I remember being so terrified. There I was, propelled at speed away from the sunshine and happy seaside noise into the sulphurous darkness of the tunnel.

As I sat helpless in the little car, gruesome apparitions reached out towards me. Blood-stained hands, evil faces, skeletons and cold, clammy things that brushed against my face. I couldn't move, I could not even scream for help, I just looked up in the general direction of Heaven and a miracle happened. Suddenly a window opened high above and light streamed down into the darkness. A face with a pipe in its mouth grinned at me, it was the man who controlled all the switches and levers and who was in charge of all the horrid apparitions that frightened me so much.

'Get me out of here,' I wailed.

'It's all right luv,' he replied, ''cos I'm 'ere wiv yer.' At the flick of a switch he could have stopped the train and transformed the darkness into light, but he did not need to do that. Just knowing he was there in control made all the difference, I almost enjoyed the ride after that.

Sometimes events, or the fear of what might happen can seem like those ghost train 'nasties' coming at me from every side. No one understands because I cannot explain how terrible I feel. But my treasure of darkness is to remember that the 'man who controls the switches' is

---

Oh Lord, may I be content to know that goodness and mercy shall follow me without wanting to see them in advance of me. George Matheson

there with me, even when I can't see him through the darkness.

'I have set the Lord always before me; because He is at my right hand I shall not be shaken.' (Psalm 16:8)

God is not only with us, but He does something to help

God tells us not to worry 365 times in the Bible – 'fear not', once for every day of the year but there are two ways of saying 'don't worry'.

I remember standing at my cooker one day while the sweat positively poured off me, the potatoes needed mashing, the table was not set and the mound of dirty saucepans was overflowing the sink. Any minute all my in-laws would be arriving for a birthday meal and I was behind schedule.

'Don't worry,' said a friend, who had 'just popped in' 'Why ever are you working yourself up into such a state?' she added as she lay back in the comfortable arm chair and slowly lit another cigarette. I felt like killing her!

'It's easy to say "don't worry" when she has no

Worry on the part of God's children is unconscious blasphemy, when we fret we are saying, 'God, You aren't in control of this situation'. David Watson

---

Anxiety is the natural result when our hopes are centred in anything short of God and His will for us. Billy Graham

intention of lifting a finger to help me,' I fumed as the custard boiled over the stove.

Just then my husband arrived home and as he walked into the kitchen he said,

'Don't worry.' What a difference! He intended to help me. 'I'll take over in here,' he said calmly, 'You go and set the table.' When God says 'don't worry' to us, He says it in the way Tony did. 'Don't worry because I'm not only here with you, but here to help you.'

Transferring the worry

The thing I find so hard is the actual transfer of the worry from my head (or should I say stomach?) into the Lord's hands. I can pray about something at great length and then get up and go on worrying about it all day, while I burn the toast, forget appointments and generally render myself useless. I find I have to make that transfer a practical, visual thing. So I keep my mother's old Bible permanently open in my workroom. When a worry even looks like swamping me I write it down on a piece of paper and I place it on the open page of the Bible. Then pointing to it I say;

'There it is Lord, lying in your hands.' As I turn my back on it and go away I find I can leave it behind me mentally as well. Of course the old familiar butterflies keep coming back because I am the worrying kind, but I have to keep on fighting them every time by saying, 'Lord, that worry is now your responsibility.'

And the peace of God which transcends all our powers of thought, will be a garrison to guard your hearts and minds in Christ Jesus. Philippians 4:7 Weymouth

Distraction helps

While the worry is lying there in God's hands the best way I have found to fight the 'butterflies' is by doing something else which is physically and mentally absorbing.

Martin Luther was constantly engulfed by anxiety and the depression which can go with it. His coping strategy was this:

'When I am assailed with heavy tribulation, I rush out among my pigs rather than remain alone.' On another occasion he said; 'I exorcise the devil when I harness the horse and spread manure upon my fields.' Fortunately most of us will not have to do anything quite as smelly as that, but turning out drawers, cleaning the car, or weeding the garden might be just as effective.

Why doesn't God make all Christians placid and easy going?

Of course God could easily do that, but He has a special love for nervous people. Remember Gideon and Timothy? While God's strength shows up best in weak people (2 Corinthians 12:9, LB). His peace shows most in born worriers! It has never been the easy-going, self-confident people who have 'cut much ice' in the King-dom of God. It is the temperamentally nervous and deeply sensitive people who often know God best. We meet God at our weakest place, and if you are the kind of person who always ruins today by panicking about the tiny details of tomorrow, that is the weak place where

> *Jesus said 'Fear not', therefore it must be poss-ible and is made possible by acting as though one were not afraid.* Basilea Schlink

you will meet God constantly. Placid people only worry over the big traumas of life, so they do not feel the need for Him so often.

Successful worriers can train themselves to turn to God frequently as each worry hits us, and by doing that we learn to know his special consolations. 'When anxiety was great within me, Your consolation brought joy to my soul,' says Psalm 94 verse 19, NIV. The Psalmist's joy came through meeting the Lord *in* his anxiety, and not by having it removed.

I am the Lord, I do not change. *Malachi 3:6, LB*

9: THE DESERT CAUSED BY OTHER PEOPLE

'I went to work on the staff of a Christian Holiday Centre, and was horrified by the way 'senior' Christians behaved when they weren't 'on show'. If knowing Jesus doesn't really change people all the way through, I felt there was little point in continuing to be one.'

'Our lovely Church was split apart by a silly human power struggle. People I thought were my friends

---

The worst evil one has to endure is the anticipation of the calamities that do not happen, and I am sure the thing to aim at is to live as far as possible in the day and for the day. Lord Beaconsfield

suddenly took sides and said bitter things about each other. We haven't known the Lord for long and we were horrified that Christians could behave like this.'

'When I discovered that the friend who led me to the Lord, and our (married) vicar were in love and seeing each other a lot, my faith was shattered.'

These are what I call 'deserts of disillusionment', and I have come across a tragic number of them this year. Perhaps the trouble is that we have extremely high expectations of our fellow Christians. It is easy for us to accept that we sin and can be forgiven ourselves, but we find it almost impossible to forgive other Christians, especially when we admired them greatly and have moulded our lives on their influence. We tend to think our leaders must be supermen, treat them with awe and put them on pedestals but when we discover they were only human after all, we feel disillusioned.

'Don't put your trust in human leaders', says Psalm 146 in verses 3–6: 'No human being can save you . . . Happy is the man who . . . depends on the Lord His God the Creator of heaven, earth and sea.'

We have lived through a revolution during the last few years. For many of us, Church is no longer a place to visit for an hour on a Sunday, it has become our close family circle. We rely on each other, share our deepest feelings and submit to authority in a way that would have been unimaginable a few decades ago. That is wonderful, and how Jesus wanted his Church to be. Yet taken to excess, it can be dangerous. Men have always found it easier to

---

Nothing has ever come to me, nothing has ever gone from me, that I shall not be better for God by it. A. B. Simpson

worship something they could see than to follow the invisible Jehovah directly. God cannot tolerate idolatry and when we put our Christian friends and leaders higher in our estimation than our God, that is idol worship.

Church splits

Many Churches are splitting these days. The pain can only be appreciated by people who have been unfortunate enough to live through the experience, but there are 'treasures of darkness' even in this agony. Division often leads on to growth, not only in cells and border plants but also in churches. God allows these painful experiences to teach us to trust Him alone. Could *your* desert have been caused because you were relying on a human being more than on God Himself?

'Several of us decided to leave our Church when we felt the Leaders simply wanted to dominate people's lives like power-hungry sharks,' said Liz and Mike, 'but we felt so lost we didn't know where else to worship. So for a while, we met in our house, but it soon developed into a "grudge-sharing" session.'

They felt they had lost their identity when they left their church, their status in their community, friends, security and even their opportunity for Christian service. But they had not lost God Himself. Discovering that was their 'treasure of darkness'.

I have a problem with pedestals, I tend to put people on them, when God wants to be there alone. Hester Dain

Before Liz and Mike could settle peacefully into a new church they had to ask God to help them forgive the people in their previous fellowship, and also to give them the courage to ask forgiveness for the pain they had caused them by leaving.

Whose fault was it really?

'Nothing anyone can do to us can injure us, unless we allow it to cause a wrong reaction in our own spirit,' says Amy Carmichael. Sometimes we feel our desert was caused by the selfish cruelty of someone else. The driver who drank too much and killed our child; the man who elbowed us out of the job we so much enjoyed; the husband who left us to cope with the family alone. These people may have caused our misery, but secretly we know they did not cause our desert.

Our inability to forgive

It is our inability to forgive which separates us from God. 'If you forgive others the wrongs they have done to you, your Father in heaven will also forgive you. But if you do not forgive others, then your Father will not forgive the wrongs you have done.' Matthew 6:14–15

Margot's father was a tyrant who clouded her childhood in misery and his malevolent influence followed her into her adult life. When he died, he left his affairs in a cruel trust that shackled her permanently to her old home so full of unhappy memories.

Whoever says that he is in the light, yet hates his brother, is in the darkness. 1 John 2:9

'I felt chronically angry with him as the years went by,' she told me, 'always my resentment of him was at the back of my mind. I carried on going to Church on a Sunday, but gradually all the joy and reality of my Christian life died. Inwardly I knew I had lost God. One day a friend said something to me, quite out of the blue, which made me furious.

"You'll have to forgive your father, you know, this anger is destroying your life." I totally ignored the comment and "dropped" the friend completely. Some years later I was persuaded to go on a Church pilgrimage to the Holy land at Easter. I only went to please someone I was very fond of at the time. Something strange began to happen to me on Good Friday. I stood watching the pilgrims from all over the world carrying their heavy crosses up the Via Dolorosa and the tears just streamed down my face. The thought of Jesus struggling along the same road broke something inside my heart. If He could forgive such cruelty, why could I not forgive my father? At long last I was willing to be made willing to forgive, but somehow I just couldn't do it by myself. On Easter Sunday I was standing by Lake Galilee, and I actually met the risen Jesus. I didn't see Him, but I know He literally confronted me, and I asked Him to forgive my attitude and help me to forgive my father for damaging my life. I have never been the same since, and my relationship with God is now the centre of my existence.'

Perhaps from time to time, it would do us all good to ask God to help us make a list of anyone we need to

---

She could have loved them if it had occurred to her to ask for the grace of God. Elizabeth Goudge. From *The Rosemary Tree*

forgive. 'Get rid of all bitterness, rage and anger with every form of malice. Be kind . . . to one another, forgiving each other as in Christ God forgave you.' (Ephesians 4:31–32)

Persecution

'My husband didn't seem to mind when I first became a Christian. He said it was only a craze that would pass, like jogging.' Christine told me. 'But when he realised how important it was becoming to me, he started poking fun at me all the time, making negative little comments about my Christian friends and criticising the Church. I'm beginning to see things from his angle now, and I wonder if Christianity is really worth the hassle.'

'The Bible says you must be glad about this,' I told her. 'Because it makes you one of the élite group of Christians and you'll have a special reward waiting for you one day.'

'What do you mean?' she demanded.

'You are being persecuted,' I replied. 'Not thrown to the lions or burnt at the stake – dramatic persecution like that often strengthens people marvellously. It is far harder to live permanently with subtle persecution, as you are.'

When you are surrounded by people who constantly pour scorn on your faith and Christian involvement it is very hard not to go into a 'desert of doubt'. It is tough never to feel accepted in the group at work, school or college and to be the butt of every joke. An even more

---

It has always been easier for Christians to be thrown to the lions than to be laughed at.
Tom Rees

difficult situation to handle is persecution by other Christians.

'When I was baptised in the Holy Spirit,' said Kevin, 'people at church felt I had been carried away with new-fangled ideas. I could feel old friends pulling back from me. I was even asked to stop teaching my Bible Class. It was easy at Spring Harvest to be bubbling with joy, but after a few months back in our Church, I was beginning to think I had made rather a fool of myself until I suddenly realised I was caring more about what people thought of me than what God thought.'

Persecution is never pleasant
The Bible says:

* We must expect to be persecuted. (Matthew 10:22–23)
* Be glad about it because of the reward involved. (Luke 6:22–23)
* We have to pray for those that persecute us (Luke 6:28)
* and express our love to them in practical ways. (Luke 6:35)

Coping with cruelty
One day I received a letter from Kelly who was really suffering at the hands of other people. Her boss browbeat her, her elderly mother-in-law (who lived with them) bombarded her with constant irritating comments and:

God teaches men through suffering and uses distress to open their eyes. Job 36:15

My husband criticises everything I do, and disagrees with everything I say. We don't argue verbally, but our spirits clash all the time. It's my inner reaction to all this that bothers me. I'm always simmering with silent rage, and that makes me feel guilty when I come before God.

I spend my time grovelling on my knees asking God to forgive me and then almost at once their comments 'get to me' yet again.

I sat in front of my keyboard for a long time wondering whatever to say in reply, and feeling sure I would fail totally in trying to cope with a situation like this. Then, suddenly I realised it was three o'clock, my favourite time of the day. Each afternoon I get into my electric wheelchair and go off to meet Richard from school. That day, however, it was so stormy that the rain seemed to be hitting me horizontally! If it had not been for my storm cover I would have been drenched. It is a huge waterproof Red-Riding-Hood cloak that envelops me and my wheelchair completely.

I had been reading Psalm 18 verse 2 that morning, 'The Lord is my protector . . . and with Him I am safe, He protects me like a shield; He defends me and keeps me safe.' As I battled along I thought to myself grimly, 'I need more than a shield like a dustbin lid to keep me safe in this storm.' Then I realised that in fact my storm cover was far better than an old-fashioned shield; it wraps round me completely, just as God enfolds me. I knew then how to answer that difficult letter. After a hot cup

In the shelter of Your presence You hide them . . . in Your dwelling You keep them safe from accusing tongues. Psalm 31:20

of tea, I did my best to describe my storm cover to Kelly.

'When we let Jesus envelop us completely, the unpleasantness of others falls upon Him, like the rain, but it cannot get through to damage us.' I wrote, and then added a quotation by R. Leigham which says: 'What can harm thee when all must first touch God, with whom thou hast enclosed thyself?'

Kelly replied a few weeks later, saying; 'When they all start on at me now, I put God between myself and them, and it works wonderfully.'

For I am overwhelmed and desperate and You alone know which way I ought to turn. *Psalm 142:3, LB*

10: THE DESERT OF UNCERTAINTY

These are horrible deserts, with no roads or signposts, just irritating goat paths that look promising at first and then peter out into an empty expanse of sand.

'God has blocked the way and I can't get through, He

One day, in my distress, I prayed fervently . . . Then all of a sudden, it was as if the finger of God was pointing not at the other person, who was causing me such distress, but at me. 'You are the one who has to change.' Basilea Schlink

has hidden my path in darkness.' says Job in Chapter 19 verse 8.

I met about ten people this year who were lost in a desert like this:

> I feel as if the secure structure of my life has crumbled away, leaving me vulnerable and emotionally homeless. People who know where their lives are going and what God wants of them can say such maddening things from their position of security. All our friends have different opinions on what we should be doing but only the Lord really knows and for some reason, He just isn't saying.

Brian Woodgate describes these deserts as, 'walking the plank blindfolded. Every time you reach the end and think you're going to plunge into disaster, you find the plank has lengthened a few more inches.'

I shall never forget Beatie's pinched, white face as she sat opposite to me, trying so hard not to cry.

'We were sure God wanted us in full-time Christian service. We had the green light through several verses from scripture as well as the opinion of mature Christians. God could so easily have stopped us, but we sold our house easily and found a lovely new one near the Missionary Society headquarters. The four kids were all settling happily into new schools when everything went wrong. Working in an office with Christian people was not what my husband thought it would be, personalities

> *I will lead my blind people by roads they have never travelled. I will turn their darkness into light . . . these are my promises and I will keep them without fail*. Isaiah 42:16

clashed, and after three months he had to resign. That's when my desert began. I kept wondering if we had mistaken the Holy Spirit's guidance in the first place?

'We don't know what to do now. We can't afford the mortgage to stay here and anyway my husband can't find another job, so we felt we were supposed to move to a cheaper area to be near our parents, but again – no sign of a job, and this house has been on the market for over a year now. What is God playing at with us? I could understand all this if we had wilfully gone against the Lord like Jonah, but we only wanted to serve Him.

'The one thing that helps is this verse someone gave me. I've stuck it on my dressing table mirror. The Lord says, "I will teach you the way you should go. I will instruct you and advise you." (Psalm 32:8) That's a promise and I know God never broke one yet! But I have to confess,' she added grimly, 'It's taking me all my time remembering that!'

Don't forget the battle of the super powers
Satan and God are both trying to do something different in these agonising deserts. God wants to teach us to trust Him in the face of human reason. He has a perfect plan for our lives, organised in detail before the world began. It is His responsibility to reveal it to us, but He never does that all at once, just step by step because He wants to teach us to walk 'by faith and not by sight'. We cannot know, love or please God until we have learnt to trust

---

Faith is a poor thing if we cannot trust in the dark, whether we understand or not. Canon Guy King
It is the darkness which makes faith a reality. Bramwell Booth

Him in the dark. Until He tells us what to do next we must do as George Macdonald suggests and 'Fold the arms of faith, wait in quietness until light goes up in the darkness.'

Another of God's objectives is to develop patience in our lives, but the only way this fruit is ripened is by adversity and frustration. 'Dear brothers, is your life full of difficulties and temptations? Then be happy for when the way is rough, your patience has a chance to grow. So let it grow, and don't try to squirm out of your problems. For when your patience is finally in full bloom, then you will be ready for anything, strong in character, full and complete.' (James 1:2–4, LB)

Satan on the other hand is working hard to use all this confusion and frustration to hurt God badly. He knows that if we panic, and begin to doubt God's ability and desire to care for us, God will be deeply hurt. In this desert Satan can also indulge his favourite hobby – condemnation.

'You must have got it wrong as usual,' he says. 'God didn't really tell you to move . . . change your job . . . come to this college . . . marry that man. How pre-sumptuous of you to think God Almighty should guide a worm like you.'

The very first time we read about Satan in the Bible he is trying this game on Eve.

'*Did* God *really* tell you not to eat fruit from any tree in the garden?' He sneers. He did it to Jesus too, in His desert. '*If* you are the son of God . . .' in other words, 'you could be wrong'.

The only way to survive Satan's constant battering is to do

Thou camest not to thy place by accident – it is the very place God meant you for. French

as Jesus did. He simply met Satan's sneers with scripture. 'If . . . ?' said Satan.

'It is written,' replied Jesus.

Beatie was doing just that when she stuck that verse on her dressing table mirror and clung to her promise against her earthly common sense. One man I heard about recently wrote out on a large piece of paper the promise God gave him from the Bible and 'took possession' of it each morning by standing on it before he got dressed.

We can rely on God to prevent us from making a mistake when we genuinely want to walk the path He has planned for us. If we keep on trying one little goat track after another He will certainly stop us every time we set off in the wrong direction. 'The Lord is compassionate and when you cry to Him for help He will answer you . . . If you wander off the road to the right or the left you will hear His voice behind you saying here is the road, follow it.' Isaiah 30:19–21

What happened to Beatie?

My mother had a favourite little ditty which went: "The God who taught me to trust in His name, would not thus far have brought me to put me to shame.' I could not help remembering those words when I had a letter from Beatie recently.

Eventually they *did* sell their house and found a new one right in the heart of the country. Her husband *did* find a job and the children all settled into excellent schools.

> *If we are desirous of living in God's will, He will not allow us to get out of it by a small mistake on our part.* Fred Mitchell

'Best of all is our new Church,' she writes. 'We have always been a bit traditional in our worship, but this Church has recently come into renewal, and the people have a joy and a freedom we knew we wanted the moment we walked through the door . . . We feel as if our outward shell of Christianity has been smashed by all the trauma we went through and inside we are now warm pliable putty in the hands of God. This experience has changed our whole lives and all the misery and confusion has been worth it, just to be here.

One Sunday night in our new Church I reflected how nearly I had given up on God. But inside my head He said, "would I so lightly give *you* up?"'

Chaos at the airport

I once discovered a wonderful Treasure of Darkness in a crowded airport terminal. We had to meet a friend who was coming to stay with us during a very unsettled and confusing patch in our lives.

'This place looks like I feel,' I remarked rather crossly. Fog had delayed flights and caused utter chaos. People were swarming anxiously in all directions, not knowing what to do next. I saw one poor man dashing round behind a trolley piled high with luggage, the perspiration was running off his face, but on his back in a carry-seat his baby slept peacefully, oblivious of the pandemonium going on around him.

'It's all right for some!' I smiled, then I remembered a verse I had read that morning, 'Let the beloved of the Lord rest secure in Him for He shields him all day long

> *God's deliverance does not come* from *trouble, but* in *trouble. He offers victorious living, not whimpering back door escapism.* Dr Crossip

and the one the Lord loves rests between His shoulders.'
Deut. 33:12. That baby trusted his father to get him home
on the right plane and to satisfy all his other needs, but I
had God for my father, He knew the way He was taking
us through the shambles of our lives. We did not need to
strive and wrestle with our problems; we could rest
between His shoulders and relax. As Corrie ten Boom
said, 'Don't wrestle, nestle.'

**Jesus said; 'But the time is coming . . . when you
will be scattered . . . leaving me alone. Yet I will not
be alone, for the Father is with me.'** *John 16:31–32,
LB*

11: THE DESERT OF LOSS –
LONELINESS AND BEREAVEMENT

'I went into a desert when I lost . . .' so many of my letters
start like that.

'All my children seemed to leave home about the
same time, making me feel redundant.'

'We moved house and I missed the support of my
friends at church, especially my prayer partner.'

Others mentioned the loss of a job or a responsibility.

---

*The Lord Himself will lead you and be with you. He
will not fail you or abandon you, so do not lose
courage or be afraid.* Deuteronomy 31:8

'Without a job to get up and go to, I felt devalued and I thought God must feel the same.'

'We had to watch the vision we felt God had given to us destroyed by other Christians.'

Some people mentioned the loss of their health, youth and good looks – the middle-age crisis, or the emptiness that retirement can create. Some even felt they had lost something they had never actually possessed.

'I wanted to be married, have a home and kids, but it never worked out, and I feel bereaved.'

'People thought I was silly grieving for a baby I had never actually held in my arms.'

The most poignant letters of all were from those who had lost people they loved through rejection or death. Any kind of loss can leave us staggering under a deep sense of desolation which also destroys our self-confidence and makes us feel unsure of where we fit into the universe. The joy has gone out of our lives, which easily leads us to imagine that God has left us too.

What is really happening above our heads?

Satan likes to see us lose the people and things that we love. When we feel shattered, rejected and empty, he hopes to encourage us to feel bitter as well. His one fear is that we might fill the gaps left in our lives by a deeper relationship with God.

I depend on God alone; I put my hope in Him. He alone protects and saves me. Psalm 62:5–8

On the other side, God is *not* gloating over our misery, He yearns to be allowed to pick us up in His arms and comfort us. Naturally He never snatches other things away from us but when, through the normal course of human life, they go, He longs to fill by His love the emptiness they leave behind. So often these people or activities have actually been more important to us than God, so He waits anxiously to see if at last we will make Him the centre of our existence.

'My husband was such a wonderful man,' said Ivy wistfully. 'So good at knowing what to do, and he was such a good Christian too; he had the faith for both of us. When he died I was knocked for six. For months I was in one of your deserts and it had no signposts, paths or landmarks. Then I gradually came to realise that for years I had had no need of God at all. I hadn't looked to Him to provide for our needs. It was Tom's good job and clever investments. It was not God who guided us in our major decisions, it was Tom's common sense. Suddenly I was alone, all the decisions were mine to make, and I had no ability to make them, I *had* to trust God, for perhaps the first time in my life, and turn to Him over every detail.

'When Tom was there I didn't need God's company either, now I'm alone I hate having no one there to hear me say, "I think I fancy a nice cuppa." So I started chatting to the Lord instead. Oh, if only I could describe the joy I've found in coming to know Him as a friend.'

Sometimes He takes away that which is most precious so that into the void of a life that is utterly broken He may pour the glory of His indwelling love. Dr Alan Redpath

It sounds trite to say 'fill the gaps with God', but when that advice comes from people who have discovered the truth of it during the worst moments of their lives, it makes you feel it is worth taking.

When the police came to tell me Jack had been killed, the silly thing was that all could think about was a couple of lines of a hymn. 'From the best bliss that earth imparts, I turn unfilled to thee again'. The words kept ringing in my ears for days, and somehow they showed me in which direction to run – towards God.

'God is actually the only person we can be perfectly sure we shall never lose,' wrote Elizabeth who lost her husband and small daughter in a car crash. 'Everything and everyone else in life can fail you, leave you or let you down, but God – never!'

Danger! desert hazard

Beware of filling the gap with something else. Pascal, the philosopher once said, 'In every human being there is a God-shaped hole that only He can fill.' When we try to fill that void with something or someone else we stay in our desert.

Perhaps the loneliest woman I know lost her husband about six years ago. In her grief she turned all her attention to her teenage son.

'She worships that boy,' people used to say, and they were right, but her possessive need of him smothered the boy entirely and he could not wait to leave home. He hardly bothers to keep in touch now.

> *Thy presence fills my solitude.* Longfellow

Cardinal Wolsey worked for Henry VIII with all his energy, but when he was a frail, frightened, old man who expected to be executed at any moment, he said, 'if I had served my God as I have served my Prince, He would not have left me thus.'

There is nothing wrong in enjoying the people or activities God sends to enrich our lives, but if they become idols, greater in importance to us than God himself, our happiness is in jeopardy. So often the harder we cling on to people the more likely we are to drive them from us in the end. Clinging to God brings everlasting security.

The secret sorrow you cannot share

Hilary never really minded being single. She had a close friend with whom she shared hobbies, holidays, and shopping expeditions, yet there was always the privacy of her home to enjoy. It was a happy relationship.

Then, for some unexplained reason, Hilary's friend drifted away, found another companion with new interests and the relationship died abruptly. Hilary felt completely desolate. She had relied on her friend for spiritual support and strength as well as fun and companionship. If it had been a husband who had left her, people would have rallied round and comforted her, but this was a private grief she could not share.

'One day,' she told me, 'I realised I had reached a crossroads, I was certainly in a desert, but there are

---

Can I be fully the person I should be while remaining single? I decided I could be – otherwise God is not God. He chose my circumstances and must mean them for my good. Hester Dain

always crossroads in the desert, you can decide to go towards God or away from Him into secret bitterness. I chose to go towards Him, even though, since the loss of my friend He had become so cloudy and dim. The old Authorised Version of the Bible seemed dry and unhelpful, so I went out and bought myself a new translation. It was so refreshing, it bought the whole thing to life for me. Suddenly I found myself in the middle of a springtime love affair with the Lord Himself. It was indescribable. Strangely, a short while later, He sent along a replacement friend, but since then my deepest relationship has always been with Him.'

Sorrow and bereavement

It seems from my letters that bereaved Christians are more vulnerable to the tactless blunders of other people than any other desert traveller – and most bereaved Christians do go into a desert at some point within the first three years.

I would hate to add to the stack of trite sayings, because so far this desert has not been one through which I have had to go. So I will let these people speak for themselves.

'Time heals', everyone tells you, but it doesn't, you just learn to live with it.

You feel oddly angry when birds sing, people laugh and flowers still bloom, your world has stopped, how can the rest of the universe be so insensitive?

> *Let me not be afraid to stand alone, for if only I will turn from other people and look for You, You are always there.* Mary Hathaway

When my son died, at the age of ten, I felt furious with people who tried to comfort me with little texts. They all seemed to be in the future tense.

'He *will* suddenly remove the cloud of sorrow . . . *will* destroy death for ever . . . *will* wipe away the tears from everyone's eyes.' Is. 25:7–8 All those future *'wills'* were no help to me, when it was *now – this minute* that hurt so much. Believing in a future Heaven does not save us from the pain, grief and tears of this present life. So it is useless for us to try and pretend that death is not an outrage, however prettily we dress it up by calling it 'resting in peace', or 'going home'. It certainly *is* all that and infinitely more to the Christian who dies. To those of us who are left without them, it is nothing but an agonising experience of loss, when it brutally drags away from us someone we love and *need*. However close we may be to God we cannot really expect to recover from the pain of that blow in this life. All we can know for certain is that we shall recover one day when God finally destroys death.

One day a card arrived with a verse written inside which actually was in the present tense at last. 'Even though I walk through the valley of the shadow of death, (in the deepest darkness) I will fear no evil for you *are* with me.' Psalm 23:4. Now I just hang on grimly to those words, 'you *are* with me', and gradually I am discovering that He comforts *now* as wells as in the future.

When I look beside me, I see that there is no one to help me, no one to protect me. No one who cares for me. Lord I cry to You for help, You Lord are my protector. Psalm 142:4–5

One day I was sitting in the armchair in Brian's old study, surrounded by his books and missing him unspeakably. Because he had been the vicar, I felt I lacked someone whose responsibility it was to comfort me! Brian was always so loving towards widows. Idly I picked up a book and noticed it was called *Pastoral care of the Bereaved*, and I almost dropped it again in disgust. Then, suddenly I noticed a passage that Brian had marked heavily. It had obviously been so important to him that I looked at it more closely.

As I read these words I felt Brian himself was speaking to me, saying the very things he would want me to know if only he had been here. Needless to say, I found them indescribably comforting.

'There is NO getting over sorrow, but there is getting into it, and finding right in the heart of it the dearest Human Being – the Man of Sorrows Himself. I pray that you will never get over it, but through it, right into the heart of God.'

All Your waves and billows have gone over me, and floods of sorrow pour upon me like a thundering cataract. Yet day by day the Lord also pours out His steadfast love upon me. Psalm 42:7–8

> And He (Jesus) is the head of the body, the church
> . . . so that in everything He might have the su-
> premacy. *Colossians 1:18*

12: THE DESERT ASSOCIATED WITH LIFE IN A CHURCH COMMUNITY

It might surprise Church leaders to know how many
people feel their deserts are caused directly by the
Church itself. Some people wrote to tell me they felt their
church was either too cold, lukewarm or just too hot for
comfort.

The cold church
This letter comes from Vivian, who was delighted when
her family moved to a cottage in the country, but:

> There is no alternative to the Parish Church. It's very
> picturesque, but the people all go along because it's the
> thing to do – a village institution. It smells of musty
> hymn books, woodworm killer and damp plaster. The
> services are dreary and divorced from everyday living,
> and all the congregation seem to care about is who's
> allowed to do the flowers or clean the brass.
> When I read about other Churches where people
> actually expect God to intervene in their lives, I feel like
> a child outside in the cold, looking through a window
> at someone else's party.

---

*Jesus turned water into wine, sometimes the
Church manages to turn wine into water.* David
Watson

Because there is absolutely no alternative for Vivian, I suggested that perhaps God wanted her there, in that situation, to show people that God is very much alive. By the same post I received another letter from someone I greatly admire and I sent a copy of it to Vivian.

I have attended our Parish Church for thirty years now and never once have I heard the gospel preached from the pulpit. I have wept, fasted, prayed, stumped round our fields with the dog or knelt in my prayer cubby hole – nothing, no change. But I have not died of thirst. Psalm 84 verse 6 says, 'As they pass through the dry valley of Baca, it becomes a place of springs'. My 'springs' in the desert have been the books I read, magazines, and tapes I listen to, conferences we attend and the little prayer group in the next village. I know I am where the Lord has put me, so I can trust Him to keep me going. G.

Vivian found that letter very helpful.

The lukewarm church

This is what Gordon said about his church:

Actually neither of us wants a Charismatic Renewal, but we've begun to feel oddly frustrated by our Church. I look round at them all on Sunday mornings, good solid evangelicals, steeped in Bible knowledge

---

Forget the former things, do not dwell on the past, see I am doing a new thing! Now it springs up, do you not perceive it. I am making a way in the desert and streams in the wasteland. Isaiah 43: 18–19

and thoroughly worthy activities. Living on the religion of our godly parents or basing our existence on some blessing we received long ago in our teens. But everything happened 'yesterday' and I catch myself feeling, 'surely Christianity isn't supposed to be this dull'. Some of our friends have left and gone to a more adventurous Fellowship ten miles from here. Naturally their names are mud round here, but we can't help privately thinking how alive their faith has suddenly become. We don't really know what makes this other place tick, and we are not sure yet, if we have the courage to go and find out.

When the Jews had walked right over their desert they stood looking across the Jordan at the Promised Land. It was still only a few months since they left Egypt, but they were too scared to march into a new situation. Sadly God had to allow them to wander back into their desert for forty long weary years. If your pillar of cloud is leading you on, into a new land, do not be too frightened to follow. Edward England once said, 'By holding onto yesterday's adventure, we miss what God has for us today.'

The church that feels too hot
Gayle, who is a very shy, quiet person said this:

I tried very hard to enjoy the House Church that my family and all their friends attend, but I felt exposed

> We try to domesticate the Holy Spirit and use Him like the house cow, we like to confine Him inside the walls of our Church, for our own benefit. Jim Graham

and embarrassed. When I went to university I found an Anglican Church and I discovered a new peace in contemplative prayer. I have always found it easier to worship through classical music, so I love the organ and choir, the order and dignity of the traditional services and beautiful surroundings make me feel safe. I know the folk in our fellowship at home think I have gone into a desert, but really I have escaped from the one I was in for so long!

God has given us a choice

Recently we spent a day in Kew gardens which contains the world's biggest collection of plants. Some flourish in hot humid greenhouses, like steaming jungles, others bloom in dry desert heat, some like marshy bogs and plenty of shade, others prefer the cool rocks of the alpine house. All the plants do well at Kew because all their different needs are met. Just the fact that they are all plants does not mean they should all blossom in the same environment. Just because we are all Christians does not mean one type of Church is right for us all.

We feel upset by the many denominations into which Christ's body is split, but I am sure He has allowed it in order to provide us with different ways of worshipping to satisfy our varying temperaments. I happen to like spontaneity, exuberance and a good beat to the music, but the services I like would deafen Gayle's spirit. Deserts begin when we try and force ourselves to stay in the wrong kind of environment, simply because we have always gone there to please other people.

Why do we find it so hard to change churches

Perhaps, like Gordon you genuinely feel that your Church is holding you back from God, yet you find it hard to think of moving to another.

'I couldn't possibly leave this Church,' you say, 'I might lose my friends.' But are your friends more important to you than getting out of your desert and restoring your relationship with God?

'I don't want to upset and hurt people.' God might need them shaken before they will start to realise something is missing in their lives with Him.

'I've been a member here for so long, it's a question of loyalty.' The church is the body of Christ world-wide. Of course we owe our loyalty to that body, but it is not contained exclusively in one little building down our road. By staying, you may be bolstering up something that is not honouring to God, a group of people from which His spirit has departed, but they are far too busy running their organisation to notice.

Danger! Desert hazard

Beware of becoming a spiritual nomad. Some Christians spend their lives wandering aimlessly from one Church to the next in search of the latest excitement to liven up their dry souls. Nomads are doomed to a lifetime in the desert because God wants us to settle down and be committed and submitted to one identity group. Often it is responsibility that nomads are trying to escape. They look for a Church that will do something for them – provide a well organised social programme, excellent music, comfortable buildings – it never occurs to them that God might be asking them to give, as well as receive. Many Churches are crying out for people to man their Sunday Schools, visit and care for the sick and elderly and organise support for missionaries. It is often by

> *Do not trouble about anything but loving Him, never mind if you cannot see Him.* Francis Malval

doing something for God that He becomes real to us again.

Desert of stagnation

The Dead Sea is a lake in the desert full of impurities and chemical deposits. Why? Because the river Jordan flows in at one end and nothing whatever flows out of the other. It is the lowest point on the earth.

We can listen to sermons, read Christian books, attend Bible studies and conferences, but if nothing ever comes out at the other end we are in a desert of stagnation.

Ministry burn-out

'I suffered from a chronic inability to say the word 'No'.

'I dreaded Sundays. By the time I'd dashed round madly fixing someone to do the crêche on Wednesday morning, nabbed people to make quiches for the Harvest Supper and organised lifts for the Youth Group outing, I was too harassed and exhausted to worship.'

'I saw a programme on television about Africa. A certain tribe had over-farmed their land, never giving it time to lie fallow or feeding it fertiliser. They had produced a desert. I thought, that's me! I'm too busy to listen to God, my prayer life is nothing but a series of gasps for help as I gallop to the next assignment and I only read the Bible in order to work up talks for other people.'

> *No amount of activity in the King's service will make up for the neglect of the King Himself.*
> Robert Murray M'Cheyne

If our christian activities are becoming more important to us than God himself, perhaps it is time we gave them up.

Could your desert be caused by:

* too much giving and not enough receiving,
* too much talking and not enough listening,
* too much doing, and not enough being?

Has God taken you into this desert to say, 'Be still and know that I am God?' Psalm 46.10.

Working for the wrong boss

I wonder if God ever feels like asking, 'Who are you doing all those jobs for – yourself or Me? Amy Carmichael says, 'Are you doing your chosen work for God, or His chosen work for you?' There is a very big difference. When God asks us to do something for Him, He also gives us the strength and ability. When we do something just because we think we might do it rather well, or we feel it is expected of us or simply because it needs doing, it can become the burden which causes a desert. A need does not constitute a call. God would rather *not* have a job done than see you in a desert because of it.

Professional Christians

Many Christians become too heavily involved simply because everyone wants to feel valued by others.

> *If you are never alone with God, it is not because you are too busy, it is because you don't care for Him, don't love Him and you had better face the facts.* A Ghazzali

Perhaps we are secretly quite proud of the many jobs we do so tirelessly for God, our success makes us feel like a better Christian. It was not always like that, of course. We might have felt helpless when we first took over the Youth Group, but we prayed earnestly for God to help us in our utter weakness, and He did! In fact He helped us so much we began to think, 'Really I'm quite good at this, I've got a real gift with these youngsters, look how big the group has grown since I took it on.'

'You're doing a wonderful job,' people tell us admiringly, but when we allow professionalism and self-confidence to rob God of his rightful glory we sentence ourselves to a secret desert of which no one else is aware.

One of the nastiest deserts in the Bible happened to Nebuchadnezzar. He stood on his roof garden and gloated over his beautiful city of Babylon.

'I have conquered the world,' he thought, but he refused to admit it was God who had made him great (Dan. 4:24–37). His pride caused seven years of mental illness. No psychiatric hospital for him, Nebuchadnezzar was driven into the desert, where his hair grew long and wild as did his finger nails, like the claws of a bird. It was not until he 'praised the supreme God and gave honour and glory to the One who lives for ever' (Dan. 4:34) that he escaped from his desert.

Of course God wants us to take on responsibilities in His Kingdom, but it is His power that achieves the success, so when we fail to give Him the honour He might well withdraw that power and leave us looking very small and silly. Deserts are terribly humbling places, as Nebuchadnezzar discovered.

If Satan cannot make us lazy or sinful Christians, he will make us proud of the fact that we are neither! Tom Rees

The real reason we go to church

There is no such thing as a perfect Church this side of Heaven, but real worship has nothing whatsoever to do with the other people in the pews, the buildings, or the form of worship.

Once when the Church we attended was right in the middle of a most unpleasant patch of squabbling and upheaval I found myself wondering, 'whatever do I go to church *for* anyway?' It took a great big plumber with a ginger beard to show me my treasure of darkness. He was a neighbour of ours and every evening he came lumbering home, down the crowded street, clutching his tools and his lunch box. His little three-year-old daughter would watch from their window, and as he turned the corner she ran down the busy pavement like a rocket on short, fat legs.

'Daddy!' she would shout, 'I found you a caterpillar, for your tea'. As he knelt down and enveloped her in his arms, they were both oblivious of everyone else, locked together in a private world of happiness and all the time she talked about the little happenings of her day she had a delightful way of stroking her father's cheek.

I thought of those two when I heard David Pawson preach on a tape from Zechariah Chapter 7 verse 2. He told the story of the men of Bethel who came to Jerusalem 'to pray for the Lord's blessing', He told us that the Hebrew for that phrase actually means, 'to stroke the Lord's face'. In Church, I worship God by coming eagerly into his presence, like that little girl, so that I can be close

---

So then stand where you are and you will see the great thing which the Lord is going to do. 1 Samuel 12:16 *Don't just do something, stand there.* Jamie Buckingham

enough to 'stroke His face'. It is simply a fusing together of my soul with God's spirit, regardless of other people or anything else.

Set my spirit free that I might worship Thee,
Set my spirit free that I might praise Thy name.
Let all bondage go and let deliverance flow,
Set my spirit free to worship Thee.

Author unknown. From *Songs and Hymns of Fellowship*, Kingsway

8

DANGER IN THE DESERT

> The Lord will make you go through hard times, but He Himself will be there to teach you and you will not have to search for Him any more. If you wander off the road, you will hear His voice behind you, saying 'Here is the road. Follow it.' *Isaiah 30: 20–21*

Poisonous snakes, scorpions, and running out of petrol are some of the hazards of life in the Sahara. Spiritual deserts also have their classic dangers.

Spreading your desert

'They were driving me mad,' said Jeremy, 'sitting round on the floor, Bibles open on their laps, smug smiles on their faces. Christian jargon spouting all round the room. I wanted to shake them out of what I suddenly felt were their cosy delusions, so I waited until our House Group Leader asked if anyone had anything to share, and then I let them have it. I suppose I

> *When any fit of anxiety or gloominess or perversion of mind lays hold upon you, make it a rule not to publish it by complaints but exert your whole care to hide it; by endeavouring to hide it you will drive it away.* Dr Johnson

exaggerated my negative feelings for dramatic effect, but I was sick of being a hypocrite – pretending everything was still all right when it wasn't.'

When we are suffering in our desert the desire to shock other Christians can be very strong. We want to use our pain as a weapon to make others suffer, and because we are so angry with God we want to hurt Him by destroying the faith of people He loves. While it can be a huge relief to talk in public about our deserts, we are actually in danger of doing Satan's job for him by spreading our doubts far and wide. If you catch 'flu it is always kinder to go to bed than to breath your germs about in the cinema. Doubts are just as catching as 'flu, and often just as short-lived. Jeremy, the 'angry' young man in that House Group was fine again after a week at Spring Harvest, but three of the people who heard his outburst that night never came back.

Of course we need to talk openly to someone, we badly need prayer, love and advice. It is *who* we talk to that matters. A small group of mature and prayerful Christians can literally carry us through our desert and they will not relax until they see us safely out at the other side. We must talk honestly to them, but it is never fair for us to relieve our feelings in front of weaker Christians, if by doing so we jeopardise their faith.

There is no need to lie
'So what am I supposed to say when people at church ask, "Are you all right?" Do I invent a lie?'

No – you could be much more subtle than that. Say, 'The Lord is doing wonderful things with my life. I'll tell

Don't cherish your doubts. Douglas McBain

you all about it soon.' You may not believe what you are saying, but it does happen to be the truth.

A desert in the family

Some of the most tragic letters I have received this year were from people whose husband or wife is going through spiritual desperation.

'He's moody, snappy with the kids, and nothing I say or do seems right,' wrote Fanny. 'You walk in through the door and a thick cloud of gloom hits you in the face.'

Of course when we are really clinically depressed we probably cannot help ourselves, but when we are merely 'feeling down' we must fight constantly not to allow our 'moods' to lower the joy temperature of those around us. We have no right to pull them into the desert of despair with us. I found a prayer by Dr Leslie Weatherhead which has often helped me on gloomy days.

'Help me O Lord so to strive and so to act, that these things which cloud my own way may not darken the path which others have to tread, give me unselfish courage so that I am always ready to share my bread and wine, and able to hide my own hunger and thirst.'

Beware of decision making in the desert

'I'm feeling drained by all these Church responsibilities, I think I'll just chuck the lot.'

Never act in a panic, be still, wait upon God until He makes known His way. So long as that way is hidden it is clear that there is no need of action. Dr F. B. Meyer

'I'm a hypocrite, being a House Group leader when I feel so far from God.'

In a desert we feel like quitting everything, and Satan loves our letters of resignation. Perhaps we are ever more drastic, 'I'm getting out of this job,' we say, 'selling this house,' or 'leaving my wife'.

Stop! Danger!
Satan would love to make the desert an opportunity to curtail our work for God and ruin our lives permanently. The basis of our decision-making as Christians is our trust in the Lord and close contact with Him. If for some reason we have lost those, we might easily make a mistake if we do something hastily while we are still in the desert.

Duncan was two when I lost him in Woolworths. We kept missing each other as we ran round searching among the counters. After that day we made a rule that if he was lost, he was to sit down on the floor and wait in the place where he last saw me. Unless circumstances force us into action we are better to stay quietly in the place where we last saw the Lord.

Of course the mature Christian, who is counselling you, may insist that you take a temporary break from Christian leadership in order to receive ministry yourself. You may well need space for a while, but avoid permanent, life-changing decisions.

The irrevocable change
About seven years ago I remember talking to a friend of mine, a minister who I now realise was in a desert.

Faith is a willingness to trust God when the pieces don't fit. Katie Wiebe

'How can I stay in the ministry when I suddenly can't believe a word I'm preaching?' he demanded miserably and resigned. When I was researching for this book I asked him if he still felt he had made the right decision. He looked at me sadly and replied,

'If only I had realised then how short these wretched patches are! I regained my faith very soon after I had gone into secular work, but by then we had lost our home and changed our whole way of life. I should have stuck my head down and sweated it out and I would have come out at the other end with a renewed and strengthened vision. I feel as if I have been wandering aimlessly ever since.'

'Wouldn't it have been wrong to pretend you were all right when you weren't,' I ventured.

'I could have put other people "up front" whose enthusiasm was high, and simply kept pegging on in the background quietly,' he replied. 'Because I admitted I had doubts so publicly the faith of many people I had led to the Lord was shaken or destroyed. Perhaps most people who work for God have bad patches but I would advise them to stay put and wait for the storm to pass, because it does.'

A recipe for hypocrisy?

'If we are in trouble and we do not feel we have enough faith to meet it, we should *act as if* we did.' Those words were written by Pascal the seventeenth-century mathematician and theologian and at first sight they look like gross hypocrisy. Should we act the part of a Christian, even when we don't feel like one?

Hypocrisy means pretending to be something which

You can't feel your way into actions, but you can act your way into feelings. Selwyn Hughes you are not, and however you happen to feel just now, you are still a child of God, so you are being honest when you act like one. If one of the Queen's sons became mentally ill and secretly thought he was a tramp, it would not be hypocrisy for him to go on living in Buckingham Palace, launch a ship or open a new hospital. However he feels inside cannot alter the fact that he is still a Prince. It may be an 'act' to act as if we are a Christian but is it not an 'act' of faith?

It began to worry the young John Wesley that he was a busy clergyman while inwardly he had no real faith in God's salvation. He was advised to:

'Preach faith until you have it, and then because you have it, you will preach it.' Pascal's 'Act As If' method certainly worked for John Wesley.

'Good spirits which are first simulated become at length real,' says Sir Walter Scott.

The hazard of synthetic praise

'My dear,' cried a friend as she breezed through my door one morning, 'I have a word from the Lord for you.' My heart sank, I was deeply depressed and sick of people with hot lines to Heaven. 'Your attitude is negative,' she beamed, 'start praising and thanking the Lord for this situation.' I did just manage to stop short of murder. 'What right has she to say that?' I fumed, 'her life's not shattered.'

People will probably have told you to start thanking the Lord, too, or peppered you with books on the power

---

How God rejoices over a soul which surrounded on all sides by suffering and misery does that upon earth which the angels do in Heaven, namely loves, adores and praises God. G. Tersteegen

of praise. Actually, not many people in the Bible thanked God loudly until *after* their trouble were over. Elijah wanted to die in his desert (1 Kings 19:4). When David's baby son was ill, the king refused all food and spent the nights lying face downwards in prayer on the cold floor of his bedroom (2 Samuel 12:16). Job complained bitterly and Jeremiah acidly enquired, 'Do you intend to disappoint me like a stream which runs dry in the summer?' (Jeremiah 15:18).

Of course when we can thank God in and for our troubles, miracles begin to happen – Jonah's fish deposited him safely on the beach and Paul's prison was demolished by an earthquake. However, for most of us, exuberant praise is not an automatic reaction under stress.

Over the last decade, perhaps many deserts have been caused because people felt crushed by guilt and condemnation when they were unable to praise God loudly in the face of tragedy. God knows we are human beings, and it is not a sin to feel sad when our child dies or when we are badly hurt. He does not expect us to thank Him glibly for allowing it, He only longs that we will turn towards Him in our pain and by doing so enable Him to bring good out of ugly situations. Jesus wept for Mary as she stood by her brother's grave, He did not condemn her for not saying 'thank you'.

Paul and Silas certainly praised God loudly in their prison, but Peter went quietly off to sleep in his, yet he too, escaped. When we put our hand into God's hand and trust Him silently for an impossible situation, that is just as much a form of praise as singing hymns loudly.

Praise is not so much thanking God for what has happened, as trusting Him for what is going to happen. John Sherrill

The danger of turning to idols

The Jews had reached the most ghastly point of their desert. Moses had left them. It was over a month since he had walked up that great rumbling mount Sinai and disappeared in clouds of thick smoke. He was certainly dead by now. Here they were – stuck! They'd be killed if they went back to Egypt and killed if they went on to Caanan, stay here and they'd die too – of thirst and starvation. All those fairy stories about God! Moses must have made them all up!

It was no wonder they were miserable, and what did they do? Just what we do when we are tense, depressed, bored, or generally 'fed up'. They looked for comfort.

'We need a nice pretty god we can see, touch and enjoy, like the ones they had in Egypt,' they said, and made a golden calf.

When we feel we need a way of escape we 'drown our sorrows' by over indulging in whatever is our congenital weakness. Food, drink, smoking, sex (either in reality or vicariously through video nasties, porn, sexy books or

---

*I cannot say, beneath the pressure of life's cares
   today,*
'Joy in these';
*But I can say that I had rather walk this rugged
   way*
If Him it please.
S. G. Browning

---

*Happy are those who trust the Lord, who do not
turn to idols or join those who worship false gods.*
Psalm 40:4

trashy television). Of course we do not really find comfort – like the Jews in their desert, we only add guilt to our misery.

God has not abandoned us any more than He had left the Jews. It is to Him we need to keep on turning for comfort when life feels shaky, and not to the idols of this world, however attractive they may appear.

The hazard of crowds and noise

When God is trying hard to tell us something we do not want to hear, it is easy to hide from Him in a crowded church or a busy home. We can even keep our minds so busy with the noise of modern life that He has no chance to reach us. We have a television set in the lounge and bedroom, a radio in the car and cassette player in the kitchen, but are we drowning out God's voice by constant noise?

God had to take Elijah away alone into the Desert of Sinai before He could speak to him in His 'still, small voice'.

If you are the kind of person who tends to take life as it comes, accepting people and situations as they are, without trying to change everything, deserts can be very dangerous. As the folk song says, 'I've been down so long it seems like up to me'. We can get used to feeling flat and dull and accept without thought a less than satisfying Christian life. Sometimes we have to shake off that lethargy by doing something drastic.

> *The dearest idol I have known, what e'er that idol be,*
> *Help me to tear it from Thy throne and worship only Thee.*
> William Cowper

Many people who wrote to me described the turning point of their desert as a definite time when they went away alone with God, with the firm intention of 'sorting themselves out before Him'.

'I packed a picnic,' said Betty, 'and I said, "Lord, I don't care if you speak to me or not, I just want to give you my undivided attention for once." I didn't really pray, but I thought through the whole of my life as I walked over the Downs. It was that day which got me out of the wretched limbo I had been floating about in for so long.'

Other people escaped their deserts by attending Bible weeks, conferences or pilgrimages. 'I booked two nights in a bed and breakfast,' said one person, while others went on a supervised retreat in a community, with counselling, fasting, and silence.

Time is our most precious possession, when we are willing to give God our day off, a weekend, even our precious annual leave and go away in order to listen to God in silence, we are saying, 'I care *this much* for our relationship, I want to get it right again'.

The danger of forgetting other people exist

'Stop feeling so sorry for yourself and start thinking of other people for a change.'

'*Ouch!*' Doesn't it hurt when well meaning people say that? I don't know about you, but my own misery became

> We need to find God, but He cannot be found in noise and restlessness. God is the friend of silence. The more we receive in our silent prayer, the more we can give in our life. Mother Teresa

like a hood that settled over my head blinding me to the
needs of others.

'Don't tell me your troubles, I've enough of my own,'
says the folk song, and really when we are staggering
under the load of our own problems we feel someone
else's would certainly be the last straw which flattens us.
Yet the Bible tells us that is not so.

> If you give food to the hungry and satisfy those who
> are in need, then the darkness around you will turn
> to the brightness of noon . . . your wounds will be
> quickly healed . . . you will be like a garden that has
> plenty of water, like a spring of water that never runs
> dry.   (Is. 58:10–11)

Have *you* ever felt surrounded by darkness?
Wounded? Or dried up like a garden in drought? God's
promise is to all of us who feel like that, but the condition
is that we divert our attention from our own misery and
start caring for other people.

This is actually how Jesus Himself coped with the
agony of His crucifixion. He healed the lacerated ear of a
man who came to arrest Him, he cared about the women
who watched Him struggling up to Calvary and as He
hung on His cross He arranged for His mother's future,
and the comfort of His best friend John. He even had time
to reassure the dying thief beside Him.

Job pitied himself for more than thirty chapters of his
book, but when at last he was able to pray for his
irritating, friends, God released him from his desert. (Job
42:10)

---

*We are never so near to God, as when we are
telling someone about Him.* David Pawson

Peggy is a farmer's wife from Somerset and her desert was long and dreary.

I noticed a remarkable thing. Every time I was filled with despair, doubts or a sense of inadequacy, the Lord reminded me of someone even more in need than I was. When I could manage to pray for them, I began to feel better. If I popped in to see them, or asked them round for a coffee, I found myself talking about a faith I do not feel as if I felt it, and a God who seemed far away as if He was as close as ever. I got all excited about the things I was telling people and as I listened to myself talking I came away feeling far more cheered and comforted than they were. When I use people as a waste paper basket for my fears and doubts the problems seem to grow bigger.

I did not dare to write to Mother Teresa and ask her if she had ever been in a desert! If I had, she might well have reminded me of something she once said;
'We all long for heaven where God is, but we have it in our power to be in Heaven with Him right now – to be happy with Him at this very moment. But being happy with Him now means; loving as He loves, helping as He helps, giving as He gives, serving as He serves, rescuing as He rescues.
'Be a living expression of God's kindness; kindness in your face, kindness in your eyes, kindness in your smile.'

There may be times when you cannot find help, but there are no times when you cannot give help.
George S. Meniam

9

DESERT SURVIVAL

My whole being follows hard after You and clings closely to You, Your right hand upholds me. *Psalm 63:8, AMP*

In desert warfare, if you can manage to cut off or jam your enemy's lines of communication, you can relax and leave starvation and dehydration to do your work for you. No one survives in a desert without fresh supplies. Satan is a cunning 'desert rat', so the first thing he always tries to do is stop us communicating with God. He makes church uncomfortable, Bible reading boring and prayer virtually impossible. But are we going to let him? This chapter is mostly a collection of the ways some people managed to keep in contact with God even 'under fire'.

'The Bible is boring'
'There's no point in reading the Bible, when you don't get anything out of it,' says Satan, but God has told us that the Bible is:

> *My teaching will fall like drops of rain and form on the earth like dew. My words will fall like showers on young plants.* Deuteronomy 32:2

* More important than our daily bread (Deuteronomy 8:3)
* It is a lamp to light our path (Psalm 119:105)
* More precious than all the money in the world (Psalm 119:72)
* The sword with which we defend ourselves (Ephesians 6:17)

Duncan, our son, had mumps extremely badly! I did not insist he ate steaks and suet-pudding, I gave him just a few mouthfuls of something nourishing every couple of hours.

'This milk-shake tastes like sawdust,' he complained.

'Never mind,' I replied, 'You must swallow it down however it tastes, because it will give you the energy to fight the germs.' A desert is really an illness of the soul, just as mumps is a physical illness. Naturally we cannot take huge chunks of Romans or long chapters from Revelation, but our spiritual 'milk-shakes' are vital.

'After our little Hannah died,' wrote Carol, 'I couldn't cope with my usual daily Bible reading notes, it felt such a grind. So I just went to certain passages I know and love, bits of the Bible that fitted my feelings at the time. When I was at my worst I just managed one verse a day.'

Carol's letter gave me the idea of making a collection of short passages that might help people in various deserts. You will find them at the back of the book under 'Desert Rations' (p. 205). It is of paramount importance that we

---

If your law had not been the source of my joy, I would have died from my sufferings. Psalm 119:92

keep on listening to God daily through the Bible even when He appears not be to saying anything to us at all.

'I couldn't read for myself,' wrote Joan, 'but Phillip would read aloud to me, and then give me one verse to hold on to all day; he used to write it on a card, which I propped up on the mantelpiece.'

Another coping strategy came from Sandra:

I bought one of those tear-off calendars from the Bible bookshop with a text for each day. I had it in the kitchen, somehow it made me realise God can speak to me even while I do the ordinary jobs of every day.

When Church is impossible

'The first reaction to any wilderness is withdrawal,' says Jamie Buckingham and most of us would agree with him.

'The hymns bring back too many memories.'

'I used to feel part of the "in crowd", now I feel at the very back of the "out crowd".'

'If you don't leap for joy in the aisles in our church they all want to take you apart and dissect you. I just want space.'

These are a few of the comments I have heard and the Psalmist adds, 'I am like a wild bird in the desert, like an owl in abandoned ruins.' Psalm 102:6. Whoever heard of a flock of owls?

When we feel least like going to church, that is the time when it is most vital to go. Tom Rees

As we have already seen in Chapter Two, Satan loves to separate us from other Christians. If you slice off your finger it can be stitched on again, provided you arrive at the hospital quickly. Leave the thing lying around for a few days and no surgeon in the world could help you! As Christians we are part of a body, and like the finger we can survive a short separation from formal Church services but never a long one. The gap between our deciding not to go and the withering of Christian life is short. Here are some ways people coped when acute depression or trauma made Church impossible for a while.

'Church was too full of sympathetic people, but our little Tuesday evening prayer group was my lifeline,' said Alice.

Ruth told me, 'I made myself go to Church after Denis died, but I never went there on Sundays! I crept in during the week when no one was about. I knew I needed God, but He was so maddeningly intangible, I had no assurance that He was there, but I was in a consecrated building that had been used by generations of people who needed Him, so I used to sit there in a pew, not praying, just sitting there in God's house. It helped so much that, after a while I managed to stay for the small Wednesday morning Communion Service. Again, no feeling of comfort, but going forward to the Communion rail and holding out my hands to receive the symbol of Christ's body was like a physical joining. I needed something concrete like that. I'm a practical, down-to-earth person.'

> *Sometimes when things are at their worst, you simply have to grind through, step by step, clinging to the Lord as hard as you can.* Maggie Boon

Sylvia said, 'After we lost our son, formal worship was impossible for a while, so I spent a whole summer of Sundays going on long rambles alone with God. I poked around under the stones in a stream and watched all the tiny creatures He made in such perfect detail, or sat on top of a hill looking into the far distance. It made me see my own problems in perspective. If God could make all this, He could certainly help me with the small and the large things that frightened me so much. Worshipping Him like that mended the parts of me that had been damaged and when the winter came I was happy to go back to church again.'

What the Bible tells us about Church

* We are commanded not to 'give up the habit of meeting together, as some are doing. Instead let us encourage one another.' (Hebrews 10:25)
* As Christians we need to follow the example of Jesus. 'On the Sabbath day he went as usual to the synagogue,' (Luke 4:16)
* God wants us all to feel we 'belong'. 'He sets the lonely in families.' (Psalm 68:6, NIV)

If we go on going to Church even if we don't feel like it, we are at least being obedient. If we decide to give up and watch a video instead we are less likely to hear God's voice.

How clearly the sky reveals God's glory! How plainly it shows what He has done! Psalm 19:1

Martin Luther, who frequently suffered from bouts of depression, wrote in his diary; 'At home in my own house there is no warmth or vigour in me, but in the Church when the multitude is gathered together a fire is kindled in my heart . . .'

Praying when prayer is impossible

So much has been written about prayer, that it amazes me that most of us still find it so difficult! Few great men are as honest as David Watson when he says, 'There are times when I almost give up the battle of prayer altogether and have to trust God's grace and faithfulness. When I am in these seasons of depression the Lord seems a million miles away.'

Praying in the desert can feel impossibly hard. How many of us have felt like saying this to God?

If I try to pray my words bounce back off the ceiling and I feel embarrassed at talking to myself. Sometimes I do not want to find You, it's too disturbing. But God, you would rather I brought the turmoil of my thoughts to You than use them as an excuse not to pray. Whether I want to or not I must find You, for without you life has no meaning and I cannot rest until I reach You.

I found that prayer in a book written by Mary Hathaway, who lives in constant pain. (*Peace Be Still* – Lion Publishing)

The essential act of prayer is to stand unprotected before God. What will God do? He will take possession of us. That He should do this is the whole purpose of life. St John of the Cross

Are we all trying too hard? Perhaps we think we have to work through a spiritual aerobics routine every morning when all God wants us to do is to sit for a while and listen to Him.

Prayer does not always need words

Recently I was watching 'Songs of Praise' on the television, when a vicar allowed himself to be interviewed, just two weeks after his wife had died of leukaemia.

'During your wife's illness did prayer help?' he was asked.

'Yes,' was his reply, 'but not in the way you might think. At a time like that prayer is more an attitude to life than a recitation of set words at the same time each day. It is just resting on God – taking Him for granted.'

Here are a few extracts from the letters I received.

'Praying feels like talking to a man who is watching a cricket match!' said Denise.

'I didn't want to pray when my husband died,' said Maureen, 'and no words would come, but I made myself sit in my chair for a while each morning. I wasn't confessing, praising or begging, just sitting there with God. I used to breathe very deeply, and tell myself I was breathing *out* all my tensions and worries and breathing *in* God and all His peace.'

We live in days when the emphasis is on extempore prayer, but when our own words fail us, here is some

---

But as for me, I will pray to You, Lord; answer me God, at a time You choose . . . because of Your great love, because You keep Your promises to save. Psalm 69:13

good advice from Sister Margaret Magdalene from her book *Jesus: Man of Prayer*. 'Liturgy comes to our aid in times of great spiritual darkness and aridity, when we can dredge up nothing from inside ourselves. It enables us to jump into the great river of prayer that flows ceaselessly to the Father and be carried along in it, when we do not feel like praying at all.'

The more difficult prayer is the more precious it is to God

Satan says, 'your silly little prayers aren't doing you or anyone else any good, why not get on with something useful?' Yet seven hundred years ago Mother Julian of Norwich wrote; 'Pray inwardly even though you find no joy in it, for it does good, though you feel nothing, yes, even though you think you cannot pray. For when you are dry and empty, sick and weak, your prayers *please Him* though there be little enough to persuade you. All believing prayer is precious to God.'

So prayer is something we can do for God's benefit, and Sister Margaret Magdalene adds to this idea by saying; 'Prayer is an offering to God and it is the offering that matters not whether we enjoy making it or not.'

Max Harper had been suffering from such severe depression that he had not been able to work for several years when he wrote to me:

I suppose when people praise God out of the overflow of their hearts, because they are happy and blessed that pleases God, but the praises of a sick

---

As a deer longs for a stream of cool water, so I long for You, O God. I thirst for You, the Living God. Psalm 42:1–2

and depressed person are far more precious to Him because they are so much harder to give.

Change your routine

'I have always prayed first thing in the morning,' said Rachel, 'but for months after the business failed I would wake in a panic. My mind would fizz like a catherine wheel, I knew I needed to pray, but prayer was totally impossible, in fact it made things worse. Activity of body helped the mental fizzing, So I used to get straight up and on with the jobs. Strangely I often found myself praying quite easily when the vacuum cleaner was going full blast.'

Perhaps Isaac Watts would agree with Rachel's discovery when he says 'little and often' is the answer to prayer in the desert. 'Do not affect to pray long. God is not the more pleased with prayers merely because they are long. It is much better to make up by the frequency of our devotions what we lack in the length of them.'

Records and cassettes of hymns and praise songs can grate on the nerves badly in some deserts, while other people find listening to sacred music is the best way to communicate with God.

Jesus prays for us

When we cannot manage to pray ourselves, Jesus does it for us. Perhaps that is the most comforting fact when prayer is being hard. 'He lives for ever to plead with God

---

But I am in pain and despair . . . I will praise God with a song; I will proclaim His greatness by giving Him thanks. Psalm 69:29–30

for them.' (Hebrews 7:25) Have you ever wondered what Jesus does these days? He is praying for you.

'If I could hear Christ praying for me in the next room,' wrote Robert Murray M'Cheyne, 'I would not fear a million enemies. Yet distance makes no difference. He *is* praying for me.'

Danger don't miss the oases

Deserts are never totally dry, every now and again you always find an oasis. We might be sitting in church, our mind a bored blur, when one phrase from the pulpit rivets our attention. A friend could make a remark or something we read may suddenly give us fresh hope.

'I'm out of this at last!' we think happily. Then a week later, when we feel just as dry as ever, we wonder whatever it was that made us so excited. 'If only I'd written it down' we think crossly.

Bedouin and their camels have the sense to preserve the water they draw from these desert springs and carry it carefully with them back out into the desolate sand dunes. Here are two ways of doing the same thing.

'I bought a little notebook,' Anna told me, 'and every time anything made any sort of sense I wrote it down with the date. When I felt bogged down in the "slough of despond" I would flip back through the pages and realise God had been speaking to me surprisingly frequently.'

Brenda said, 'I'm always at my most depressed in the kitchen, trying to cope with the jobs I can't really

---

The life of prayer is just love to God and the custom of being ever with Him. St Teresa manage any more. So I write on cards any special promise God gives me and stick it on the kitchen wall. Now after two years we can hardly see the wall for my promise cards!'

There certainly seem to be more ways of keeping in contact with 'HQ' than I ever imagined a year ago, but sometimes even these helpful ideas will be useless in the face of extreme suffering. During the terrible depression that Barbara experienced after the tragic death of her son on his motorbike, she confessed to a friend that she could neither read her Bible, pray, nor go to church. The friend replied,

'Don't you think God is big enough to cope with that? Can't He put His arms round you and hold you even when you cannot hold on to Him yourself?'

When I am surrounded by troubles, You keep Me safe . . . You will do everything You have promised. Lord Your love is eternal, complete the work that you have begun. Psalm 138:7–8

He hath more ways of hunting for our love than one or two. Samuel Rutherford

10

THE HIGHWAY TO FREEDOM

When My people in their need look for water, when
their throats are dry with thirst, then I, the Lord, will
answer their prayer, I the God of Israel, will never
abandon them. I will make rivers flow among
barren hills and springs of water run in the valleys.
I will turn the desert into pools of water . . . *Isaiah
41:17–18*

'For a long time I didn't even miss the Lord,' said Jan,
'then suddenly I couldn't stop thinking about the sheer
ecstasy I had known when I first met Him at university.
Verse 4 in Revelation Chapter 2 seemed to haunt me: 'But
this is what I have against you; you do not love me as you
did first'.

'One day I had this burning desire to recapture what
I had possessed then, so, on impulse, I parked the
children, hopped on a train and went back to Exeter for
the day. Nothing had changed as I walked round the old
familiar streets and parks, all the memories came
flooding back.'

'And did you find your first love again?' I asked her.

'I did,' she laughed, 'but I discovered I didn't really
want it any more, it had been nothing but pink, fluffy
candy floss which hadn't stood up to the pressures of
my life. I knew I needed to find a new, more durable
relationship with God. What I have now, makes my
desert worthwhile.'

I hope by the time you read this chapter your desert
will be slipping into history. Perhaps you are in that

strange 'No Man's Land', between two worlds. The activities and patterns of thought that were once your life, have been rocked to the foundations, leaving you wondering, 'where do I go from here?' The important thing, according to my friend Jan, is not to go back to where you began. It is not your old faith and love for God you need to regain. He wants your desert to be a prelude to something even better.

Beyond the desert lies a new blessing

One day God's Spirit took Ezekiel into a forgotten valley and showed him heaps of old, dry bones scattered about on the ground. 'These are my people,' God told him, 'They say that they are dried up, without any hope and with no future.' (Ez. 37:11)

Is that how you have been feeling? Just a dried, shrivelled skeleton of the Christian you once used to be? Picked clean by the vultures, useless and forgotten in the scorching heat of a desert valley? God is speaking to you, just as surely as He spoke to his people through Ezekiel.

'See I am going to make you live and breathe again, and cover you with skin. I will put breath into you and you shall live and know I am the Lord.' (Cf. Ezekiel 37:6) 'I will give you a new heart and a new mind. I will take away your stubborn heart of stone and give you an obedient heart. I will put my spirit in you and I will see to it that you follow my laws.' (Ezekiel 36:26)

As Ezekiel watched in amazement, God made those dry bones into living soldiers and they marched out of their arid valley in triumph. Are you prepared for Him to do something just as miraculous for you?

I will . . . and make Trouble Valley a door of hope.
Hosea 2:14

'But I don't feel like a triumphant soldier,' perhaps you are thinking. None of the rest of us rode proudly out of our deserts – with polished boots and a gleaming white charger. We staggered out in blood-stained tatters, but that does not mean we lost the battle. The soldier with the battle scars wins the war medal. We win when we lose our pride, sin and self-reliance and come to depend on God in complete humility. A tragically high proportion of Christians never come out of their deserts simply because they don't want to. If you have managed to crawl this far, you have won, however battered you feel!

Of course even Ezekiel's soldiers needed a road on which to march home. We too had to build ourselves a way back to God through the 'trackless wilderness', and for many of us it was very hard work.

'Comfort my people,' says your God '. . . her sad days are gone . . . make a road for the Lord through the wilderness. Fill the valleys, level the hills, straighten out the crooked paths and smooth off the rough spots in the road.' (Isaiah 40:1,3–4, LB)

In our deserts we realised just how crooked our lives had become, and with God's help we had to straighten them. We filled in the valleys of omission (by adding good things that were missing). We had to remove mountains by the faith God gave us and smooth the rough attitudes that were obstacles in our pathway back to Him.

'There will be a highway there, called "The Road of Holiness". No sinner will ever travel that road; . . . Those whom the Lord has rescued will travel home by that road.' (Isaiah 35:8–9)

> *You have put us to the test, God; . . . we went through fire and flood, but now You have brought us to a place of safety.* Psalm 66:10–12

Of course we are all sinners, for whom Jesus died, but there is no way out of a desert if we are not willing to leave our sins behind us, buried for ever under the sand.

How am I going to feel now?

The simple answer to that is – different. As I said at the beginning of this book, the desert is an experience you walk through from one side to the other and you come out on the far side a different person. 'You have . . . enlarged me when I was in distress.' (Psalm 4:1)

As I look back over my life I can remember feeling angry with God on several occasions on behalf of friends who seemed to be going through far more than their fair share of life's problems.

'Why should God allow such nice people to suffer like this?' I have so often thought. Then, perhaps years later, I meet them again and suddenly they are not just nice people any more, they have become special people. A subtle and indescribable change has taken place in their whole personalities and the way they look at life is just not of this world. Job lost everything in his desert, but after he had prayed for his irritating friends and apologised to God for his rude behaviour, God gave him back a double quantity of all he had before. Therefore, I suppose it is not surprising that God has made some of my friends into twice the people they were when I first met them.

'Jesus returned . . . the power of the Holy Spirit was with him,' says Luke 4:14. Returned from where? From His desert.

> *Give us now as much happiness as the sadness You gave us during all our years of misery.* Psalm 90:15

Are you willing to march the whole way?

After forty years wandering in the barren wilderness, some of the tribes of Israel were so pleased to see a few patches of green grass they settled down and lived in a partial desert instead of crossing the Jordan and making right for the heart of the Promised Land. (Numbers 32) Few spiritual deserts end abruptly. Things begin to improve gradually and it is tempting to relax too soon and settle down to life in the suburbs of Little Blessings, instead of marching right on to claim the Big Blessing that awaits us.

Preserve your treasures of darkness

When the rest of the Jews finally crossed the Jordan into the Promised Land, God told them to pull out from the river bed twelve great stones and set them up as a monument, to remind them for ever of all God had done. Perhaps we too, need a monument of some kind.

On my wall I have a poster, a picture of footprints disappearing into the far distance and the famous poem in which the writer asks why, if God had promised to walk with him always, there was only one set of footprints behind him? God told him that through the worst patches of his life He had *not* walked beside him, He had actually been *carrying* him! To me, that poster is a constant reminder of my desert. I also thought God had left me to walk alone, and whenever I am tempted to feel like that again, I go and look at my poster.

Naturally we want to forget our nasty experiences, but the 'treasures of darkness' we discovered are things we

---

That which had lain desolate in the sight of all who passed by . . . has become like the garden of Eden. Ezekiel 36:34–35

definitely want to preserve for ever. Could you write down the positive things you feel you have gained through this experience and keep the list in your Bible? Maybe you realise now what caused the desert in the first place. If you made a note of that too, it could work like an early warning system to help you escape, if ever you saw another desert looming on the horizon.

God even uses our deserts

One morning I was typing away at my keyboard, trying to take down everything my visitor was telling me about his desert, when suddenly his voice trailed away in mid-sentence. When I looked up I saw tears trickling from behind his glasses. 'I hate remembering it,' he said at last, 'it was all such a waste of precious time . . . time I could have spent with the Lord . . . time I should have been telling others about Him.'

So many of us feel as he did; perhaps that is why God put a special verse of encouragement into the book of Joel, just for us. 'I will restore for you the years that the locust has eaten,' Joel 2:25. A swarm of locusts can strip the harvest fields as bare as a desert, but God wants us to know He does not see our deserts as wasted, barren years, He is going to make them 'blossom like a rose'. God used Job's experience to bless him profoundly and He has also been using it to bless the rest of us ever since!

Many people who contributed to this book did not find

> *What a wonderful God we have . . . who so wonderfully comforts and strengthens us in our hardships and trials . . . so that when others are troubled . . . we can pass on to them this same help . . . God has given us.* 2 Corinthians 1:3–4

it easy to do so, but we wanted God to use our pain to help others. He will use yours too, if you give it to Him.

To show you what I mean, here are a few final extracts from letters I will value all my life.

'Pride may come before a fall, but you are a much nicer person afterwards! There are few people more useless to God than those who have never tripped over and therefore pride themselves on their consistent rectitude. William Shakespeare rightly says, "He jests at scars who never knew a wound". I came from a very sheltered background and really did tend to look down on other people. Now that my "knees" are still hurting from my fall, I understand how people feel. No one is ever going to get trite, glib little answers from me again. I've learnt to say, "I just do not know why God does or doesn't do certain things. But I do know that He knows why and that's enough for me."' Sherry

'I am beginning to see now why God allowed me to be ill for so long . . . I hope to take on a ward sister's post in the autumn and I feel a new affinity now with suffering people. I did not know what it was like for them before, and shudder when I remember how I treated certain patients. I shall never be the same Again.' Maggie

'The experience stripped us of everything else except God. It put our priorities right. The endless

Don't you think that some of us must know the trials of misty weather if we are to be enabled to understand when others are in the mist? Amy Carmichael

paraphernalia of modern life suddenly seems terribly unimportant.' Joy

'When I was going through the mill, I suddenly realised that Jesus also knew what it was like to be hassled by Satan, pressured by a family business, misunderstood, criticised and then even rejected by the people He loved best. Perhaps worst of all, to watch His life's work apparently lying in ruins. Since those things happened to me I really have come to know Him in a new and deeper way, by sharing "in His sufferings".' (Philippians 3:10) Michael

'You ask, what have I learnt through all this? Well I've discovered that happiness depends on happenings and my happenings haven't been very pleasant recently so I felt cheated. But I came to realise that happiness was not what Jesus promised us, it was joy. Like David in Psalm 51, I asked Him to 'restore unto me the joy of my salvation', and He answered that prayer as I discovered that it is possible to have joy right in the middle of unhappy events, simply by realising that God loves me, understands, and has everything under control!' Bill

'In my utter weakness I am having to lean very heavily on the Lord's arm,' wrote Peggy, 'You never learn how strong someone's arm really is, until you have to lean your whole weight on it.'

Perhaps of all the letters I received, that last one sums up the desert experience best: a time when we learnt just

> In the end *we shall see that what seemed so hindering does not hinder, but helps.* Amy Carmichael

how strong God's arm really is. 'Who is this coming up from the desert, leaning on her beloved?' says the Song of Songs (8:5). Actually there is no other way to get out of the desert than by leaning on Him, and no greater 'treasure of darkness' than to discover the full strength of His arm. Through Solomon God says to us now:

> The winter is over, the rains have stopped; in the countryside the flowers are in bloom. This is the time for singing; the song of doves is heard in the fields. Figs are beginning to ripen; the air is fragrant with blossoming vines, come then my love, my darling come with me. Song of Songs 2:11–13

You have changed my sadness into a joyful dance, You have taken away my sorrow, and surrounded me with joy. So I will not be silent I will sing praise to You, Lord, You are my God I will give you thanks for ever. Psalm 30:11–12

APPENDIX 1
DESERT RATIONS

When Jesus was in His desert He said, 'man cannot live on bread alone, but needs every word that God speaks'. It is through reading the Bible regularly that we gain strength to survive our deserts and eventually discover our escape routes. Yet, so often, when we are facing emotional trauma or physical illness, we simply cannot face reading long irrelevant passages. Here are a few of the best loved 'mini meals' to sustain you each day.

DRY, DULL PATCHES

Psalm 107:4–9
Isaiah 35:1–4
Jeremiah 17:5–10
Deuteronomy 8:2–10
Isaiah 55:1–3

Psalm 63:1–5
Psalm 36:5–9
Habakkuk 3:17–19
Psalm 42:1–5
Isaiah 55:6–11

WHEN GOD SEEMS VERY FAR AWAY

Psalm 139:1–6
Isaiah 41:9–10
Jeremiah 31:2–4
Psalm 22:1–11
Hebrews 13:5–6

Psalm 139:7–12
Romans 8:31–39
Jeremiah 29:11–13
Matthew 28:20
Isaiah 59:1–2

FAILURE, DISAPPOINTMENT AND WORTHLESSNESS

Psalm 37:3–7
Psalm 40:1–3

Psalm 31:14–22
Isaiah 50:9–10

1 Corinthians 1:26–31   2 Corinthians 4:8–9
Psalm 131:1–2   Psalm 119:81–84

STRESS, ILLNESS AND GRIEF

Psalm 143:4–8   Psalm 91:1–6
Psalm 91:14–16   Psalm 94:17–19
Psalm 73:23–26   Psalm 62:5–7
Psalm 46:1–3   Psalm 25:15–18
Psalm 23:1–6   1 Peter 1:3–7
1 Peter 4:12–14   Matthew 11:28–30
Romans 5:1–5   Psalm 121:1–8
Psalm 34:17–19   Isaiah 40:28–31
Isaiah 43:1–5   John 14:1–3
2 Corinthians 4:16–18   2 Corinthians 5:1–7
Lamentations 3:19–26   2 Corinthians 4:8–10
1 Peter 5:6–7   Psalm 71:1–8
Psalm 69:29–33   Psalm 71:19–21

WHEN WE FEEL WE HAVE CAUSED OUR OWN DESERT

Jeremiah 15:18–20   Hebrews 4:14–16
1 John 1:8–10   Isaiah 54:7–8
Psalm 130:1–6   Psalm 107:10–16
Psalm 103:8–14   Psalm 25:4–7
Psalm 25:8–12   Psalm 51:1–5
Psalm 51:6–13   Romans 5:6–11
Romans 7:24–25 and 8:1–2 Psalm 37:23–25
Isaiah 1:18–20   Isaiah 53:4–6

In Your goodness You told them what they should do; You fed them with manna and gave them water to drink. Through forty years in the desert you provided all that they needed. Nehemiah 9:20–21

APPENDIX 2
GUIDE BOOKS FOR DESERT TRAVEL

Backhouse, Halcyon (ed.), *Cloud of Unknowing*. London, Hodder & Stoughton 1985.

Backhouse, Halcyon (ed.), St John of the Cross, *Dark Night of the Soul*. London, Hodder & Stoughton 1988.

Billheimer, Paul E., *Don't Waste Your Sorrows*. Alresford, Christian Literature Crusade 1983.

Billheimer, Paul E., *The Mystery of His Providence*. Eastbourne, CLC/Kingsway 1983.

Buckingham, Jamie, *A Way Through the Wilderness*. Eastbourne, Kingsway 1984.

Carmichael, Amy, *Candles in the Dark: letters of Amy Carmichael*. London, Triangle 1981.

Christenson, Evelyn, *Lord Change Me*. Amersham, Scripture Press.

Cowman, Mrs Charles E., *Streams in the Desert*. Basingstoke, Marshall Pickering 1985.

Green, Wendy, *The Long Road Home*. Tring, Lion Publishing 1979.

Hathaway, Mary (comp.), *Peace Be Still*. Tring, Lion Publishing 1987.

Hession, Roy. *Calvary Road*. Alresford, Christian Literature Crusade, 1950.

Hurnard, Hannah, *Hinds' Feet on High Places*. Eastbourne, Kingsway, 1982.

Julian of Norwich, *Enfolded in Love*. London, Darton, Longman & Todd 1980.

Lloyd-Jones, Martyn, *Spiritual Depression*. Basingstoke, Marshall Pickering 1985.

Magdalen, Sister Margaret, *Jesus: Man of Prayer*. London, Hodder & Stoughton 1987.

Marshall, Catherine, *Meeting God at Every Turn*. London, Hodder & Stoughton 1981.

Schaeffer, Edith, *Affliction*. London, Hodder & Stoughton 1984.

Schlink, Sister Basilea, *The Hidden Treasure of Suffering*. Basingstoke, Marshall Pickering 1985.

Sjaastad, Egil, *In the Shadow of the Cross*. Basingstoke, Marshall Pickering 1987.

Warren, Ann (ed.), *Facing Bereavement*. Crowborough, Highland 1988.

Wiersbe, Warren W., *The Bumps Are What You Climb On*. Leicester, IVP 1986.